Because of a Flower

BECAUSE OF A FLOWER

Lorus J. Milne & Margery Milne

DRAWINGS BY KENNETH GOSNER

Atheneum 1975 New York

Copyright © 1975 by Lorus J. Milne and Margery Milne
All rights reserved
Published simultaneously in Canada by McClelland & Stewart, Ltd.
Manufactured in the United States of America by
Halliday Lithograph Corporation
West Hanover, Massachusetts
First Edition

Library of Congress Cataloging in Publication Data
Milne, Margery Joan Green.
Because of a flower.
Bibliography: p.
SUMMARY: Discusses various plants, such as blackberry, orchid, and milkweed, that provide centers for small communities of animal life attracted by their flowers, fruits, and seeds.
1. Flowers—Juvenile literature. 2. Botany—Ecology—Juvenile literature. [1. Flowers. 2. Botany—Ecology] I. Milne, Lorus Johnson, joint author. II. Gosner, Kenneth L., illus. III. Title.
QK653.M54   583'.04'524   74-19292
ISBN 0-689-30452-8

For Kay Sweeney, who cherishes the kampong and, beyond its acres, all of the flowering, fruiting world.

Contents

Our Flowering World 3
In the Blackberry Tangle 23
Water Lilies 35
The Extra-Special Orchids 49
The Flowers That Follow the Sun 62
The Yucca and Its Partners 72
The Flowering Oak Tree 84
Cactus Flower 97
The Many Heads
of the Foxtail Grasses 111
Milkweed Flowers 123
Everybody's Flowers 134
Flowers Everywhere 146
For Further Reading 150
Flowers in the Text 151

Flowers are an important part of our environment. They are of many different kinds. But each flower is part of a community of living things. To truly see a flower, is to see a whole community of life.

	DICOTYLEDONS	MONOCOTYLEDONS
	("Dicots")	("Monocots")
	Two first leaves in the seed; leaf veins from a branching network; flower parts in fours and fives; wood often with annual growth rings	*One seed leaf; leaf veins usually unbranched, parallel; flower parts in threes; no growth rings*

AT LEAST SOME PETALS JOINED TOGETHER

Flower with a right and left side / *Flower usually on a radial pattern*

Other flower parts fused to pistil, at least partway	Other flower parts not fused to pistil in any way

Mint family

Snapdragons

Daisies & asters (composite family, in part)

Orchid family

Morning glories

Dandelions & thistles (composite family, in part)

Potato plants

Wild carrots

Milkweeds

Honeysuckles

Blueberry bushes (heath family)

Squash plants

Petals tiny or absent; usually pollinated by wind

Oak trees
Birch trees
Walnut trees
Willow trees

Palm trees
Grasses
Sedges
Call lily
Cattail

Old Style flowering plants with separate petals

Four-o'clocks

Banana plants
Pineapple plants

Carnations
Maples

Orange trees
Sumac
Cacti

Iris
Century plants

Elm trees
Peas

Mustard plants
Roses &

Poppies
blackberries

Lilies & yuccas

Water lilies
Buttercups
Magnolias

Ancient plants 200 million years ago

Our Flowering World

> What is a common man?
>   Where is a common tree?
> I'll pick one common buttercup
>   But challenge two or three,
> For every one bears instant proof
>   Of its identity.
>
>   —Roy Helton (1886-)
>   *Come Back to Earth*

FLOWERS add immeasurably to our lives. Their beauty in color and form is irresistible. They appeal also to a great variety of animals. Hummingbirds search for flowers by day. Tropical fruit bats visit flowers at night. Many insects could not live without flowers.

What would our world be like without flowers? Long ago, it had plenty of plants but no flowers at all. It continued without flowers far into the Age of Reptiles, when great dinosaurs roamed the continents. Small birds and mammals appeared. Still there were no flowers.

Because of a Flower

Seaweeds grew in the seas. Cone-bearing trees formed forests in many places. Between the tall trees, on the ground, were ferns and mosses, lichens and toadstools. But no tree produced a fruit. Shrubs bore no berries.

Beyond the forests were no grasslands, because the world had no grasses. Without grasses there could be no grain, no wheat, no rice, no corn. Almost none of the foods that people and animals enjoy today could be found anywhere—all because there were no flowers. Flowers, when they appeared, changed all that.

Any flower can be thought of as a truly remarkable group of special leaves. They are arranged around the end of the flower stalk, in a short spiral. These special leaves fit together neatly before the flower opens, and the outer ones keep rain and insects from getting into the flower before it is ready.

The special leaves that comprise a flower are of several types. Those that are farthest down the stalk are most like ordinary leaves, and usually green. These are the sepals, which spread apart when the flower opens. When this happens another group of special leaves is revealed. Generally they are colorful, and are called petals. In

Turks-cap lily

Because of a Flower

a tulip flower, the three petals and three sepals may be so alike in color and shape as to be equally showy. The colored leaves, whatever they may be—sepals or petals—attract insects to the pollen and nectar inside the flower.

Although sometimes, one or more of the petals of a tulip flower or of a buttercup produces pollen, most of the pollen of all flowers is released from the stamens. A stamen consists of a slender little stalk with a pair of pollen sacs at the tip. Generally these rise up near the open center of the flower. The pollen sacs break open to expose the pollen grains. They are a golden dust as fine as face powder, and they produce the sperm cells of the plant.

Flowers exist to produce pollen and to get it transferred to another flower, and to receive pollen and to use it to start seeds developing. They are a plant's way of getting pollen distributed to other plants of the same kind and itself receiving pollen from other plants. Some plants depend on the wind or the rain to transfer pollen, others rely on animals. Plants that succeed in getting animals to transfer their pollen generally produce only moderate amounts. Those that rely on wind to distribute their pollen must produce prodigious amounts of this golden dust.

Our Flowering World

A plant uses up a great deal of energy in producing its flowers. It offers additional energy freely in the sugary nectar and in the pollen that is to be distributed. A small plant may have energy enough to open only one flower at a time, and to keep it attractive to animals—ready to distribute or receive pollen—for just a few hours.

Pollen grains are short-lived, too. Their separate lives begin when they are exposed to air on an open stamen. They die in less than a day if they do not reach a suitable destination. During this brief time an insect may brush against the stamen. Some of the pollen grains may stick loosely to the legs or body. But to achieve their purpose, those pollen grains must be brushed off again in the right part of another flower of the same kind without delay.

Despite their minute size, pollen grains are enclosed by firm walls. This covering is composed of a fatty material. It resists decay better than any other known product of a plant. Some pollen grains have remained recognizable for 130 million years, their coverings so unchanged that they seem fresh. Yet microscopic details in the walls of pollen grains differ from one kind of flowering plant to another. Scientists can identify

Because of a Flower

each of the 275,000 different kinds of plants in the modern world from features of the pollen covering.

The parts of a flower that receive pollen grains from other plants are at the very center. There there are special leaves that close around microscopic egg cells. Each special leaf with one or more egg cells inside is called a pistil. Usually the tip of the pistil (called the stigma) is sticky or feathery and serves to capture pollen grains. As soon as a pollen grain is caught on the stigma of the right kind of flower—its own kind—a slender tube begins to grow from the pollen grain. It grows to the nearest egg cell and delivers a sperm cell. As soon as the sperm and the egg have joined, a new plant begins to grow. The plant will be at the center of a seed. By the time the seed is ripe, the little plant inside will have stopped growing. It is an embryo waiting for suitable conditions before it grows again. When it does, we say the seed is sprouting.

The first flowers grew on trees. Some were huge magnolias, with fat green buds. The big buds opened, just as modern magnolias do, to reveal a circle of showy parts. White or creamy yellow, the flower might be a foot across.

Inside it, the plant produced droplets of nectar, which is water sweetened with dissolved sugar. And insects of long ago, just as they do today, flew to the flowers to get the nectar. After sipping in one flower, the insect might see another flower of the same kind far off, then fly to visit it next.

The plant that produces a flower, gains a great deal from the visits of animals that the flowers attract. Unlike the flowering plant, the animals can move about freely. They can see and smell where they are going. No flowering plant possesses these abilities. Without knowing what is going on, the plant uses the senses and the power of movement of the animal. The plant gains because the animal, although it does not realize it, is transferring pollen.

This service is important to the flowering plant. Transport of pollen, on a fairly direct route, with a minimum loss of time, helps insure survival of the species. And transport by animal is far more reliable than the haphazard movement of pollen by wind. Because insects often seek out the same kinds of flowers, by sight and smell, flowers whose pollen is transported by insects are most likely to receive the right kind of pollen. Then they can produce seeds and fruit.

Because of a Flower

A flower is always the beginning in the process that leads to the production of fruit. Some fruits can be eaten, and some cannot.

A peach flower has only one pistil with one egg to await the arrival of a pollen grain. When the egg is fertilized by a sperm from the pollen grain, it develops an embryo inside a single seed. Only occasionally can two seeds be found in a peach, like identical twins. The peach fruit protects them well. Close around the seed (or seeds) is the hard covering we call the pit. Next is the fleshy, juicy, sweet part of the peach, which is so delicious to eat. Around this is a skin, which may be covered with short curly hairs. The hard wall of the pit, the fleshy layer, and the skin of the peach are all produced by the special leaf that surrounded the egg cell. They are parts of the fruit. All plants with flowers produce a fruit of some kind around their seeds. The seeds of flowering plants, and the fruits that surround the seeds, are essential to the reproduction of the plants. The seeds and fruits of flowering plants are also essential foods for people and for domesticated animals. Without flowers producing pollen, and fruits with seeds inside, civilization could not exist.

We tend to overlook the pollen that insects

fruits

carry from one showy flower to another, although the fruit and seeds are well known. A pea flower, for example, has several egg cells in the single, slender pistil. When pollinated, these egg cells develop into the several pea seeds in a row, enclosed by the pea pod. The pod is the fruit of the pea plant.

Some flowers, such as those of blackberries and strawberries, have many small pistils at the center. Each pistil of a blackberry swells up to become a juice-filled bag around a single hard-shelled seed; the many bags stay in a group as one "blackberry." Each pistil of a strawberry, however, becomes a hard cover over a tiny seed; the many hard little fruits stay embedded in the red surface of the juicy "strawberry." But the juicy, delicious part of a strawberry is actually the enlarged tip of the flower stalk, with its five green sepals still attached. When an animal eats a raspberry or a strawberry, the armored seeds pass through the animal without being digested or killed. They still have a chance to grow into new plants if they fall on suitable soil and receive the right amount of rain. A fruit is a plant's way to get its ripe seeds from one place to another.

A flowering plant does not have to be a sturdy, tall tree. Plants with flowers can succeed without spending any energy in producing woody parts. Actually it is better for plants with flowers to remain low. Close to the ground, their showy parts will not be torn off so frequently by wind. Today most kinds of plants are low-growing. Many of them develop from a seed and produce flowers before getting to be a year old. No tree can do that.

Flowering plants no taller than a deer or a rabbit offer food in the form of leaves, branches and fruits to animals of this size. And these animals help the plants in return, always without knowing it. A deer accidentally steps on many small fruits and seeds. Its sharp hooves push them deep into the soil, where the seeds have a good chance to grow. The rabbit nibbles on buds and leaves, but brushes its fur against fruits with hooks; we call them burrs. These catch in the rabbit's fur and the fruits are carried along. When the hooks break and the fruits fall off, they will be far from their place of origin. There the seeds can grow to become new plants far from the parent plants. With flowers that lead to fruits and seeds, a plant can benefit from animals as though the animals were partners.

Many flowers attract only certain kinds of animals. Animals that move around in daylight are the only ones likely to visit a water lily, a morning glory, or a dandelion. These flowers open after sunrise and close again in the afternoon. You can watch their petals move, more slowly than the minute hand on a clock but often as fast as the hour hand.

Other plants display their flowers at night. The four-o'clock shows its petals late in the afternoon and closes again before dawn. The night-blooming cereus is a cactus with big flowers that open rapidly after dark. The white pet-

Because of a Flower

als may spread 9 inches across by midnight. The big, pale flower releases a sweet scent that attracts moths from far away. They come to the flower despite almost total darkness. Most flowers that open at night are pale, and you can smell their perfume.

Red flowers and orange ones are invisible at night. They attract us and animals by day. Some appeal most to bees and butterflies. Others, with the nectar deep inside, fit the slender beak of a hummingbird. The hummingbird hovers in front of the flower or below it, and reaches in to get the nectar as if it were sipping through a slender soda straw.

Flowers that are streaked or spotted with red often produce an odor that resembles the smell of rotten meat. They are wide open, and attract flies. The flies crawl around inside the flower, sipping moisture and distributing pollen. This is the way of the skunk cabbage. It is the first flower of spring. It opens on warm days while there is still snow on the ground. Flies that have survived the winter come to visit.

Scientists try to combine what they know about the long past history of flowering plants with what they know about modern flowers.

Our Flowering World

The flowers themselves are the most distinctive parts of the whole plant. They provide the basis for distinguishing one kind of flowering plant from another. Similarities between the flowers of unlike kinds of plants tell scientists that these kinds are related to one another.

During the millions of years since the first flowering plants appeared on earth, many new types have arisen. Variations occur because each seed is made by the union of cells from two different plants, which means that a young plant is a combination of characteristics from two plants. Also, sometimes, changes occur for no known reason. These are called mutations. Each new kind that survived had some advantage because of its difference. It might be able to grow in a desert or some other place that its ancestors could not have tolerated. It might have taken advantage of its new feature to spread into a different region. Usually the flowering plant then adjusted to some new way to get its pollen distributed. But the changes in the plants generally affected the flowers less than the roots and stems and leaves. Flowers change so gradually that scientists describe them as "conservative." Yet certain types of change can be noticed.

In the Old-Style flowering plants of 100 mil-

Because of a Flower

lion years ago, each flower was large and separate from others on the plant. Each part of the flower was attached separately to the flower stalk. In a magnolia flower or the flower of a tulip tree, which continue the Old-Style way, it is easy to pull down the petals separately. Often you find drops of nectar glistening on the inner surface of the petals. And there are usually quite a good many examples of each part of the flower.

Among New-Style plants, the flower parts are more definite. There are fewer sepals, fewer petals, fewer stamens, fewer pistils. If you are looking at a wild flower of a New-Style plant, there are usually four petals and four sepals, or five petals and five sepals, or some similarly low number. The flower may have only one pistil.

If the New-Style flowers are small, they are usually grouped in close clusters, perhaps like the individual flowers that comprise each "head" of thistle, dandelion, or daisy. Some flowers have lost their sepals and petals altogether; the calla lily and the poinsettia depend on some other leaf or leaves to make them showy. The calla lily gains its display from one big, white leaf, which forms a background for the slender column of minute flowers that are grouped together. A poinsettia has a whorl of red leaves around a small group of flowers, like bright flags to attract butterflies and other insects.

The parts of New-Style flowers are often joined together. The sepals may be fused along their edges, forming a cup. Or the petals are joined, perhaps to make a funnel-shaped tube, as in a morning glory or a squash flower. The stamens may be joined to the petals, and rise up from them instead of from the central stalk of the flower. Or the showy parts are joined to the pistil, at least partway. A final trend gives the flower a right side and a left, instead of the Old-Style radial pattern. We notice this in the flower of a snapdragon or an orchid, which seems to have an upper and a lower lip or other peculiar feature.

The orchids, the tulips and lilies, and the grasses belong to a great group of flowering plants that appeared for the first time only about 60 million years ago. They differ from most other flowers in having their flower parts in threes, or multiples of three. Three sepals, three petals, six stamens, perhaps, around a single pistil. The small plants in their seeds differ in having only a single first leaf (one cotyledon), instead of two, as other embryo plants have. For

large-flowered trillium and blue flag (iris)

this reason, these flowering plants are separated from all the others and called Monocotyledons or just "monocots."

Flowers that produce seeds with two cotyledons have flower parts in fours or fives or multiples of these. They are the Dicotyledons, or the "dicots." It is in such inconspicuous details that each flowering plant reveals its kinship to others. The information helps when we try to identify an unfamiliar flower. It can also be used to arrange the flowering plants on a family tree.

Our Flowering World

Today each land has its native flowering plants, and also some that have been introduced from other parts of the world. The various flowers and fruits attract many different kinds of animals. Tree flowers summon animals that climb easily or fly. Flowers on shrubs appeal to large mammals that walk about, and to flying insects that care little about the height of a flower so long as it offers something to eat. Flowers close to the ground are for lowly creatures.

By producing flowers only at a particular height, in a particular week or month, in a particular environment (such as a forest, a marsh or grassland), and in some particular part of the world, a plant can attract its own following of animals. The form and color of the flower appeal especially to those visitors that are advantageous to the plant. Only a flower that attracts the right animals will enable its kind to survive.

Each kind of flower keeps its nectar and pollen in a special place. To reach them, a bee or other animal must learn how to enter the flower. It is as if it had to learn the combination to a safe. Once it has learned this, the animal uses its time and energy efficiently if it goes to another flower of the same kind, because the same

Because of a Flower

combination is effective there. Only when the animal can find no more of the same kind of flower is it likely to investigate flowers of other kinds. Then it must learn a different way to get a reward. Because animals do tend, therefore, to visit flowers of a single kind one after another, the flowering plants gain the help they need.

Watch an active insect flitting from flower to flower in a garden. It may enter one larkspur blossom after another, resting on the blue sepals while reaching deeply into the long spur behind the small central petals. The insect gets larkspur pollen around its mouth, and transfers the pollen from one larkspur to the next.

Even if the insect has also learned how to get nectar from a blue columbine close to the larkspurs, the pollen does not get mixed. The insect alights on the stamens at the center of the columbine flower, and turns around on them while reaching into the five spurs behind the columbine petals where the nectar is located. This gets pollen on the underside of the insect. The columbine pollen would rub off on another columbine flower, but not on a larkspur. And any larkspur pollen on the insect's head would not affect the columbine, even if any did drop off.

Our Flowering World

Each kind of flower gets its own kind of pollen, because the pollen becomes attached to a different place on the animal. And this happens because each kind of flower is a little different from every other kind of flower.

To see how the community of flowering plants rewards the animals that live near by, and the kinds of communities flowers attract, we should go where they grow naturally. To find a water lily, we visit a pond or a slow part of a broad river. To spy on an oak, we go to a woodland or a forest. To watch weeds, we look in a vacant lot or along a neglected roadway. To be sure to meet a cactus, we travel to the nearest desert. In each place we discover not only the particular kind of flower we seek, but also the flowers of the other plants that grow best in similar countryside.

Close to home, we can observe the honeybees helping themselves and a great many different plants in the course of a year. In spring they buzz among the apple blossoms, gathering nectar and pollen, while ensuring a crop of apples. In summer the bees gather nectar from clover flowers, to make clover honey, and in the process help the plants produce seed. In autumn the bees have goldenrods to visit. Each flower has

Because of a Flower

a distinct relationship with the animals it attracts. Exploring these many kinds of life brings dramatic discoveries without end.

In the Blackberry Tangle

Rosalind. How full of briers is this working-day world!
Celia. They are but burs, cousin, thrown upon thee in holiday foolery. If we walk not in the trodden paths, our very petticoats will catch them.

—William Shakespeare (1564-1616)
As You Like It, Act I, Scene III

A BUMBLEBEE will go almost anywhere to find blackberry flowers. It recognizes the five white petals as soon as they spread wide apart. Buzzing loudly, it shoves its big, hairy body past stems and leaves to get at the nectar in the blackberry flower.

A blackberry bush hums as bumblebees vigorously push themselves over the many flowers. And every open flower while it is providing nectar to a bee may pick up a dozen or two pollen grains from the bee. That is how much pollen is needed to produce each blackberry

bramble (blackberry), bumble-bee

fruit. For each of the many seeds in the fruit represents a separate pollen grain.

Other insects also visit blackberry flowers. Honeybees shuttle to and fro, picking up a load of nectar and pollen, then returning to their hive. Smaller bees are less regular in their visits. They store the food they collect in small nests they have dug in the ground, or under a stone. Many of these small bees are brilliant green or blue, as though their bodies were clad in shiny metal. Often they zip straight from a blackberry flower to a nest that is only a few yards away.

In the Blackberry Tangle

The bees reveal where they are about to raise their young.

Occasionally a fly, a beetle, or a butterfly stops to get something to eat from a blackberry flower. These insects rarely travel from one flower to another of the same kind as faithfully as bumblebees. Consequently they are less helpful in transferring the blackberry pollen.

Any blackberry bush that is old enough to produce flowers is already a tangle. Its several stems arch up and over in different directions away from the central root. Each stem and its side branches are studded with sharp curved thorns. They catch on clothing and on legs and arms. An animal as big as a fox or a dog has difficulty getting through. But a chipmunk or a bumblebee is small enough to travel amid a blackberry tangle without hesitation.

The bushes in a blackberry tangle attract insects for a month or more because each bush comes into flower gradually. Often the first flowers open on low branches that are hidden from our view, but not from the bumblebee. Later the sprays of flower buds on the outside of the bush become showy. But in each spray, only a few flowers open at a time. Those at the end of the spray are the last to get ready for pollination. On any bush, wherever it grows, the flowering season extends over several weeks.

The fruits mature in the same pattern. The first to ripen come from the earliest flowers. Other fruits, toward the end of the same spray, will still be green or red. Each berry encloses a dozen or more seeds, every seed in its own little bag of juice. When the little bag reaches full size, its skin turns black and its juice winy-sweet. The seed inside is ripe and covered by an armor almost as hard as a stone. Its armor lets it resist the digestive juices of any animal that swallows it.

Delicious fruits with indigestible seeds are part of the inheritance of blackberry bushes. It is a secret strategy for life as the plant goes from flower to fruit to seedlings. Blackberries grow and flower where they do because their seeds pass unharmed through the digestive tracts of birds and mammals. First the animal has to eat the blackberry. The sweet juice in the fruit makes this worthwhile. Later the seeds reach the ground in the wastes of the animal. By then the seeds may be far from the blackberry bush on which the fruit ripened.

A blackberry seed can grow on almost any kind of soil, as long as it is well drained. That

In the Blackberry Tangle

is why you find blackberry tangles along railway embankments, where it is easy to reach the ripe fruits. Equally suitable are the gravelly materials that the glaciers of the great Ice Age left behind in many parts of North America.

The blackberry seedlings benefit from some shade. They grow well as long as the trees above them do not form too dense a canopy. Even then, roads through the forest leave a narrow gap through which some sunshine reaches the ground. Blackberries spring up along forest roads. Suitable conditions of this kind occur over most of North America, and southward on mountain slopes to the Andes.

Most of the birds and mammals that eat blackberry fruits will wait until the fruit is ripe before eating it. But they are not so particular about which kind of blackberry they find. It may be a thimbleberry, a dewberry, a cloudberry, or a wild raspberry. In the northwestern United States and nearby Canada, it may be a salmonberry, which is delicious when ripe—not too full of seeds—and pulls easily from the bush. As a group, blackberries are the number one summer food for many kinds of wildlife. Catbirds and robins become acrobats to reach blackberry fruits. Cardinals and orchard orioles,

Because of a Flower

summer tanagers and brown thrashers become blackberry addicts for weeks at a time. Pine grosbeaks and yellow-breasted chats come out of the woodlands to feast among the blackberry tangles. In northern parts of the continent, the birds get along quite well with black bears that are nuzzling through the sprays of ripening fruits, trying to pick and eat only the ripest and sweetest blackberries. In the western provinces of Canada and southward into mountain slopes and desert edges, the marmots stretch up under the blackberry bushes to reach the fruits. East of the Mississippi River, the groundhogs (which are marmots, too) pay no attention. But the cottontail rabbits find blackberry fruits an attractive change from clover and grasses. This liking for blackberries is as widespread as the bushes themselves.

Even with so many different animals coming to the blackberry tangle to enjoy the ripe fruit, some of it is never picked. Wasps that found nothing interesting in blackberry flowers will come to the overripe fruit and sip the fermenting juices. Sometimes the wasps get so much alcohol from the yeasty blackberries that they become tipsy, and cannot fly straight. Occasionally a black bear gets drunk on fermented black-

In the Blackberry Tangle

berries in the same way.

First, the blackberry flowers attract only insects. Then, the blackberry fruits appeal to animals of many kinds. Soon, the blackberry seeds are dropped all over the countryside. Wherever there is enough moist soil and light, the blackberry seedlings spring up. In the first year, they may grow only a foot or two tall. The following summer, the stems thicken and curve over. They are prickly blackberry canes, forming a tangle. Some people call it a thicket, and others a briar patch. It becomes a hiding place for cottontail rabbits. Birds build nests on the ground below the arching canes. Groundhogs dig underground apartments where the blackberry stems will keep out foxes. A blackberry tangle is like a fortress. Its hooks and thorns make it a sanctuary for wildlife that needs protection.

In winter, when nourishment is hard to find, the rabbits and deer often come to nibble on the youngest ends of the blackberry plants. In summer, the canes and leaves provide food to animals of many kinds. More than a dozen different types of insects live on or in the leaves and stems. A few others get their nourishment by boring into the roots. Several of these insects are spectacular when examined close up. Their hiding

Because of a Flower

places can be discovered through a little detective work.

The red-humped blackberry worm takes big bites out of the leaves. This spectacular caterpillar has a bright red head as well as a hump of the same color. Otherwise the body is mostly black, adorned with narrow yellow stripes lengthwise and short black spines along the back. Unlike most caterpillars, it has no paired legs at the tail end. Generally it waves this part of its body from side to side or up and down while it eats. If a bird disturbs the red-humped worm, it raises both its tail and its head away from the leaf in jerky fashion. This is a warning. Any bird that persists in coming close is likely to be squirted in the eye with a blinding jet of acid. The red-humped worm is so able to defend itself that it can move freely in plain

red-humped blackberry worm

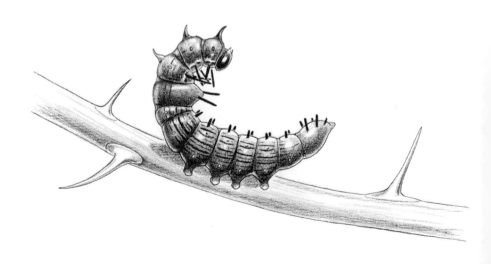

sight. A good many grow to full size—an inch long. By then, summer is over. The red-humped worm goes down to the ground. There it gathers bits of dead leaves and ties them together on the soil. This pile is a covering within which the caterpillar waits until cool weather arrives in autumn. Then the insect transforms to the pupal stage and passes the winter. It will not emerge as a moth until early the next summer. The moth, however, is seen so seldom that it has no common name. Its only protection is in hiding. Its front wings are of various shades of gray; these conceal white underwings and a black spot that marks the middle of their rear border.

The measuring worm that feeds on blackberry plants is an expert in camouflaging itself. If it is feeding on the flowers, it cuts out little pieces of the white petals and fastens them all along its back with strands of silk. If it is feeding on the fruit or leaves, it does the same with bits of leaf. Then it inches along in slow motion, holding on to the plant either with the legs at the front end of its body or those at the back end. Sharp eyes are needed to spot this caterpillar. Yet it, and the pea green moth it turns into, are found almost everywhere that blackberries grow.

Because of a Flower

A tuft of brown hair at the edge of a blackberry leaf turns out to be a very different caterpillar. Under the hairy covering, its body is almost oval. It has more legs than most caterpillars. The silken cocoon that it constructs is often noticed in winter, attached firmly to a blackberry cane. When the weather warms up, the flannel moth inside has a peculiar escape hatch ready. The moth pushes out a circular lid at one end of the cocoon and climbs out. The flannel moth's body is as hairy as its caterpillar, which makes its yellowish wings seem short. Often the moth clings through a whole June or July day beside a porch light that has been left on all night. That is the time of year when a new lot of eggs is laid, and another brood of caterpillars soon appears.

From midsummer on, the flowers of blackberries attract an unbelievable day-flying moth. It closely resembles a yellow-jacket wasp. It whirs up to the flowers for nectar, but rarely alights or crawls around. It visits other flowers as well, always behaving as though it could sting. The moth mimics the yellow-jacket wasp so well that it is rarely recognized as being something quite different. But its caterpillar does not behave like a wasp. It is the blackberry cane borer, which eats out blackberry stems while remaining concealed inside.

Anyone who has tried to make a path through a blackberry tangle knows that many of the canes are dead, dry, and brittle. Some of them are killed by insects that bore inside. Often a dying cane still contains the borer. But there is seldom any way to guess which of several kinds of insects it will be. The answer can be found only by splitting the cane lengthwise with a pocketknife. If the insect is not a blackberry cane borer, it may be the young of a fly or a sawfly or a long-horned or other kind of beetle. One of the beetles is unique in that it induces the plant to produce bumps on the outside of the cane. These are called "gouty galls," and are a good clue to what is happening inside.

The work of all these insects interferes very little with the spread of blackberry thickets. There are always plenty of blackberries for pies, jam, and wine. Every blackberry bush produces so many flowers and seeds that its seedlings spring up in most open land. They form a border around every forest in a suitable climate.

For a while, it is not easy to notice the young trees that grow in the blackberry tangle because they are small. But unlike trees in the open, they are well protected. Deer and other animals that would nibble on the young trees cannot reach them easily. Instead, the deer avoid the prickly canes. Or they browse on the softest tips of the blackberry bushes during the winter when other food is scarce. Gradually the young trees get taller and older. Their bark becomes too thick for a deer to chew. Their branches spread out. Their leaves shade the blackberry bushes. And as the forest extends itself, the blackberries disappear. The bumblebees and other animals that enjoy blackberry flowers, fruits, leaves, and canes must go somewhere else. They must follow the blackberry seeds to places where new plants are pioneering in the sun.

A blackberry flower is a sign of vigorous regrowth.

Water Lilies

What was he doing, the great god Pan,
Down in the reeds by the river?
Spreading ruin and scattering ban,
Splashing and paddling with hoofs of a goat,
And breaking the golden lilies afloat
With the dragon-fly on the river.

    Robert Browning—*A Musician Instrument*

A WATER LILY flower is somewhat like a sundial. It shows the time of day anytime the sun is bright enough to cast a shadow. In good weather, the water lily flower begins to spread its many petals early in the morning, between seven and eight o'clock. By noon it is wide open. It begins to close again for the night between one and three o'clock. By sunset it is shut tight. On cloudy days, the flower stays closed. Probably this helps the water lily keep its pollen dry by shedding any rain.

Each water lily flower inherits a schedule and

Because of a Flower

follows it closely. All of the flower parts get ready inside the bud. At this stage they are far under water, at the end of the growing flower stalk. Soon after the flower bud reaches air, it opens and has nectar to offer. But on the first day, the pollen bags on the stamens are not yet displaying their golden contents. The water lily cannot offer pollen, although it may accept some from a visiting insect. On the second day and perhaps a third day too, the flower both gives pollen and receives. The next day, only a small amount of pollen is left. This is the last time the flower will open, its final chance to get pollen from another flower.

The insects that feast among the yellow stamens of a water lily flower are mostly beetles, wasps, and bees of small size. With luck they alight like helicopters upon an elevated platform at the center of the flower. This flat landing area is solid, but scalloped and sticky around the edge. The sticky material picks up pollen from the insects as they scramble over the edge, down among the stamens. There are about three dozen stamens, but there is still plenty of room for any small insect to explore between them. The insects seek nectar, a prize that is deep in the water lily flower. Usually they get well dusted

fragrant water lily

Because of a Flower

with pollen as they try to clamber out again, on their way to the next flower.

The most handsome of the beetles that associate with water lily flowers are only about half an inch long. Their backs gleam in the sun like polished bronze. They fly so readily that they are extremely hard to catch. Often one of them backs up to the edge of a water lily leaf and stands there. It reaches under the leaf with the tip of its body, and attaches an egg where neither air nor sunshine will come. There the eggs of the water lily-leaf beetle hatch in the water. The immature beetles feed on the green tissue of the leaf. Not until they have completed their growth and transformed into mature insects will they climb around the edge of the water lily leaf into air, into the sunlight.

A water lily leaf provides many flying insects with a landing field. Dragonflies that dart about like airplanes settle singly on the dry top of a leaf. One may come to bask in the sun. Another may munch away at a mosquito or other trophy it has caught in flight. The dragonfly speeds away if a frog or a small turtle crawls out of the water onto the water lily leaf. The leaf is buoyant enough to support these small animals because it contains many spaces filled with air.

Water Lilies

A larger animal can benefit from the buoyancy of water lily leaves if it can spread its weight over several of them at once, or stand on a particularly large leaf. A bird with tremendously long toes has this special ability, although it is the size of a chicken. Known as the water lily-leaf trotter or jacana, it is native to marshes and stream edges from Texas to Brazil. It can stop or run on top of water lily leaves. But if it walks to the edge of a single leaf, it starts to sink. Then the bird must take to its wings to keep from getting wet.

The giant among water lily leaves is that of the Victoria water lily, which grows in northern South America. Often 6 feet across, with an upturned rim, the leaf will support the weight of a small child. The giant leaf does not tear easily because it is stiffened below by strong veins. Almost like girders, they radiate out from the leaf stalk.

Animals that cannot live in air often cling to the underside of a water lily leaf. Snails creep about there, grazing on microscopic clinging plants. A relative of corals, sea anemones, and the Portuguese man-of-war suspends itself below many a water lily leaf. This freshwater creature, a hydra, is as slender as a toothpick

Because of a Flower

and about half an inch long. From its lower end, six or more threadlike tentacles hang downward into the water. These are like fishing lines, extended to catch food for the hydra. Instead of bait, these tentacles bear minute nettling cells like those on hydra's saltwater relatives. The hydra uses its nettling cells to catch water fleas and other tiny animals. It subdues each victim and pushes the body into a mouth at the place where the tentacles arise. Inside is a sac-shaped digestive cavity. Any wastes are spat out through the mouth. Frequently a hydra can be seen if a piece of water lily leaf is allowed to float in a large jar of pond water. Slowly the hydra recovers from being jostled, and extends its long tentacles again.

Water lilies bear their leaves and flowers on separate, long stalks. Each leaf unfurls from a bud far down in the water. Gradually its stalk grows longer, allowing the leaf to rise upward and float at the surface. In areas where the water freezes in winter, the stalks of all the water lily leaves coil and pull the leaves down to safety when the water begins to get cold. When the water warms again in spring, the stalk may uncoil and allow the leaf to float once more. With amazing regularity the water lilies with-

Water Lilies

draw their leaves from sight and return them to the surface. These changes in the appearance of a pond or stream become signs of the seasons.

Flower buds, too, develop at the ends of separate stalks while still under water. Slowly the stalk lengthens, pushing the bud into air. After the flower has opened and closed for the last time, the stalk coils and pulls the flower below the surface again. There the petals and stamens loosen and separate from the solid central part of the flower, where the seeds are ripening. They are embedded in a pulp, and protected by a tough rind. Eventually these coverings die and decay. Then the seeds tumble out. Many of them are soon eaten by ducks and other waterfowl. Underwater currents carry a few seeds to new locations, where they may sprout the next year and start new water lily plants.

The water lily seed needs to sink to the bottom at a place where the water is not too deep or too shallow. Deep water is often stirred by big waves during storms. For days afterward it is murky, and lets very little daylight reach any plants on the bottom. Water less than 6 feet deep is too shallow for a water lily seedling. A shallow place is likely to go dry and become land during the late summer. This could be fa-

Because of a Flower

tal to a water lily plant. Its leaves must have water to float on during the warm months. Nor can the plant grow well if the current in a river is too strong. The water lily leaves will break off from the long stalks that connect them to the stem in the muddy bottom if the current pulls too vigorously.

The world has plenty of places where the water is just right for water lilies, and the water lily seeds can sprout and grow in the silty bottom. These plants live on all the great continents of the Earth, among other plants and animals that thrive under the same general conditions. Among the lily pads you can usually see small green flakes of duckweed. Dark green hanks of alga cling to the water lily stalks. Pond snails glide up and down. Dragonflies settle atop the lily pads and take off, causing scarcely a ripple. Between the lily pads, fish come up for a gulp of air, and start rings of ripples spreading. Or small black whirligig beetles produce V-shaped wakes as each swimmer zigs and zags on the water surface, searching for food. Only a scientist is likely to inquire which kind of whirligig beetle, or which fish, or which particular water lily contributes to the scene. For most people, it is enough to see the same styles of life

Water Lilies

in the Tropics, the temperate zones, or even in the Arctic. They make the world of the pond and the slow river so uniform that it feels like home anywhere. The world of the water lilies has scarcely changed for 60 million years.

A water lily seedling that grows in a favorable site puts out only a few leaves during its first year. These leaves have slender stalks an inch or two long, and delicate blades the shape of an arrowhead. With luck the young plant escapes being eaten by a bird or a fish, or by a hungry muskrat. That first year the water lily makes all the food it can with the energy of sunlight that shines down through the water to its leaves. It stores the food in an enlarging stem, which grows horizontally in the muddy bottom of the pond or stream. Every year the stem gets longer and thicker, and produces new leaves from one end. Always, however, the plant is in danger. It can be dug out by a beaver that would relish the starchy stem as food. A moose may even wade into the water and reach down until its whole head is immersed, in order to feed on the new leaves that the water lily plant is sending upward toward the surface.

Each kind of water lily probably has a distinctive taste. An experienced botanist can often tell by examining a water lily leaf which type of flower it will produce. The fragrant white water lily has circular, floating leaves that usually are purple underneath. Its flower buds commonly are purple too. Its flower petals tend to be pointed at the tips, and its stamens have stalks more slender than the bags that hold the pollen. A very similar white water lily, with scarcely any fragrance, bears leaves that are green below. Its flower buds are green. Its petals are rounded at the tips, and the stalks of the stamens are wider than the pollen sacs. People who wonder why some white water lilies are sweet scented while others are not, seldom realize that two kinds are growing side by side.

Water lilies produce flowers in most of the colors of the rainbow, but do so chiefly in the southern United States and in tropical lands. The flowers themselves resemble white water lilies, but they are purple, blue, yellow, and various shades of pink. Some flowers rise above the water as much as a foot before they open. The leaves too may be elevated, and the underside may be dry.

The common cow lilies of temperate and tropical regions have oval, floating leaves with a deep notch. Their butter-yellow flowers

Water Lilies

rarely measure as much as 3 inches across, and seem never to open fully. Actually the color is entirely in the fleshy sepals. They resemble petals so much that a person is likely to overlook the real petals. These are far down in the flower and appear to be mere scales or stamens without pollen sacs. A cow lily has an odor, rather than a fragrance. But deer wade out to eat the flowers as well as the floating leaves.

The Indians of North America have long known how to prepare food from the roots and seeds of the cow lily, which is also called the yellow pond lily or the spatterdock. Probably the Indians learned to eat the lilies by watching muskrats and ducks. Muskrats dig into the mud to remove the thick, starchy stems, then cache short pieces in their lodges. Indians rob the muskrats of the stem pieces, and make the starch more digestible by boiling or roasting. The seeds, which ducks eat, are nourishing, too. They are embedded in fruits that are egg-shaped and as much as 2 inches long. The Klamath Indians of the American Northwest collect the fruits, dry them in the sun, parch them beside a fire to loosen the rind, and shake out the seeds. If the dry seeds are roasted, they pop like popcorn, suddenly increasing in size. Usually

Because of a Flower

the Indians store the seeds and later grind them to make flour for bread.

Far larger and more famous are the seeds of the water lotus. Those produced by plants native to the Old World are called "sacred nuts." They grow into huge plants, with horizontal stems as much as 50 feet long. Their leaves rise 2 or 3 feet above the water surface. The supporting stalk goes almost to the center of the shieldlike leaf, which may be 2 feet across. The pink flowers open at about the same level. Each has a dozen or more waxy petals and a multitude of stamens around a peculiar flat-topped pistil. The pistil ripens into a strange cone-shaped fruit, in the surface of which the seeds develop in separate pockets. The whole fruit breaks off the stem and floats on the surface of the water for a month or more. Gradually the rim of the pocket around each seed rots away. The seed falls out wherever the fruit happens to be floating. This unique method of distributing seeds has helped the lotus become widely dispersed. It grows in almost every marsh along the Nile River in Egypt, in India and Ceylon, Tibet and China.

Since at least 5000 B.C., the patterns of the lotus bud and flower have appeared in the art

Water Lilies

and architecture of civilizations from China to the western Mediterranean. Lord Buddha is often shown seated on a giant lotus flower, with his legs folded in a particular way. This is the "lotus position," which followers of Zen Buddhism and yoga all over the world learn. In the Buddhist and Hindu religions, as in ancient customs of Egypt, the whole lotus plant has special significance.

The seeds of the sacred lotus hold the present record for being able to grow after a long period of inactivity. Some that were in the Hans Sloane Collection at the British Museum (Natural History) for 237 years began to sprout in 1947 when rain reached them. The water came through a hole in the roof, produced by an exploding bomb. Then it seeped through the shattered glass of the exhibit case in which the seeds were on display. Before the damage could be repaired, the seeds demonstrated that they were still alive!

America has a lotus, too, with creamy yellow flowers. Its leaves, fruits, and seeds closely resemble those of the lotus in the Old World. The American lotus grows as far north as the Great Lakes and Massachusetts, and southward into the Tropics. No mystical powers have been attributed to it. But both Indians and wild animals have enjoyed its starchy roots and nutritious seeds, each as big as an acorn. In various places the plant is known as wonkapin, water chinquapin, and pond-nut, instead of yellow water-lotus. Its foliage and flowers are as handsome as those of any other member of the water lily family.

The Extra-Special Orchids

> The purple orchid
> folds itself into itself
> discreetly. An old lady
> with a secret.
>
> —Donald M. Murray

YOU MAY THINK of orchids as rare and expensive. Yet you can find orchids flowering almost anywhere you go on land. Look for them in the shade on the forest floor, where the famous lady's-slipper orchids grow. Other kinds live in wet meadows and marshy places. One kind thrives in the bright sunlight among the short grass along a Florida highway. This orchid is less than 2 inches tall and almost as slender as a blade of grass. It lives close to the pavement, and thrives despite lawn mowers that cut off the tops of every higher plant.

Because of a Flower

To find orchids growing, you need to learn what to look for. There are many kinds of orchids, each living in some particular situation. They grow wild, high up on trees in the Tropics, and low down in peat bogs in the Arctic. Some survive on the slopes of lofty mountains. An orchid native to the island of Trinidad grows where the salt spray from the sea coats its leaves during every storm. Only the desert has no orchids.

Each kind of orchid blooms at a particular time of year. Then it produces flowers of extraordinary form and beauty. Many are exquisitely small, others spectacularly large. But until an orchid displays its flowers, it generally grows inconspicuously. In the temperate zone, orchids are rooted in the soil. But the number that put forth fine rootlets to take nourishment efficiently from the ground or extend attractive leaves are few. Until an orchid blooms, it can be overlooked quite easily.

Most orchids live in warm countries, near the Equator. They cling with stubby roots to the bark of large trees, high above the soil. Slender roots dangle from the plant into the open air. These slender roots have a special fungus covering that is spongy. It resembles lace when you

The Extra-Special Orchids

examine it through a magnifying lens. The covering serves as a trap for moisture and for dust, which provide all the minerals the plant requires. Often the stem bears short, swollen branches. The plant stores a reserve of water and food in them. The storage parts may be the most distinctive features of the orchid at seasons when it has neither leaves nor flowers. Flower buds form in the dark corners where the stem is attached to its storage organs.

Orchid flowers have many different shapes. Until about 100 years ago, no one knew why. Then Charles Darwin, the famous British scientist, began to investigate. He found that each kind of orchid flower is especially well suited for attracting some one kind of animal. Usually it is an insect—the particular kind that is the most reliable pollen carrier as it visits the orchid flowers. It may be a definite moth or a specific butterfly. It might be a wasp, a bee, or even an ant. A few orchids attract kinds of flies. Rarest of all are those that make use of visiting snails or hummingbirds. You can collect important facts about a variety of orchid without harming it, just by discovering which animals carry its pollen.

The queen bumblebees serve some of the

pink lady's-slipper (moccasin-flower)

loveliest of orchids. These are the lady's-slippers, wildflowers of late spring in the woodlands of both North America and Eurasia. Lady's-slippers blossom after the hepaticas and trilliums have dropped their petals, but before the fragile ferns spread their fronds to full size. The bumblebee buzzes directly to the center of the big bulging lower petal of the lady's-slipper flower. This petal is called the lip and has an invisible slit. The slit opens, letting the big bee disappear

The Extra-Special Orchids

inside the flower. The slit closes again, but the bee is not trapped. You can hear it buzz quietly as it crawls over the surface of the pistil. At the same time, pollen from its hairy body scrapes off and may start the orchid seeds developing. The bee goes to where the nectar is, at either side of the flower and laps up all it can find. Then the insect moves on, without having to turn around and go out through the slit lip. Instead, it can leave by one of two rear exits in the flower. Whichever one it chooses, it must pass close to a stamen. A fresh load of pollen comes off on the body of the bee. Out goes the bee, to repeat the process in the next flower.

Darwin noticed that the thirty different kinds of lady's-slippers are almost unique in giving the bee a choice between a rear exit on the right and one on the left. This kind of orchid is peculiar also in having two stamens, one beside each escape route. Other orchids have just one stamen. They require a pollen-carrier either to go out the way it came in, or to go through and out a single rear exit. In either case, the flower has its single stamen in just the right position. The stamen adds pollen to the animal before it gets away.

Orchid flowers have so many different tricks

Because of a Flower

for getting animals to carry their pollen that Darwin wrote a book about them. He entitled it *On the Various Contrivances by which Orchids are Fertilized by Insects*. People all over the world read it. Then they looked at orchids to see if Darwin's descriptions were correct. Actually they found still other tricks that no one had discovered before. Within fifteen years, Darwin heard about so many other means of pollination shown by orchids that he had to rewrite his book.

One magnificent orchid on the big island of Madagascar still keeps its secret. Its ivory white, star-shaped flowers extend toward the back as a hollow spur 10 to 14 inches long. The nectar is all at the very bottom of this long projection. Scientists believe that some animal in Madagascar reaches the nectar with a slender tongue at least this long. But what is the animal? It may be a hawkmoth. One of these moths that lives in Madagascar does have a tongue 11 inches long. But this particular moth does not fly around at the time of year when the orchid is in flower. The moth could not aid in transferring pollen. Eventually somebody is sure to discover which animal with a taste for nectar is the one for which the plant is adapted.

The Extra-Special Orchids

Each orchid does have a tremendous need to receive pollen. Its flowers will wait a week or more, wide open and receptive. Once pollinated, the flower withers within hours. People appreciate the lasting quality of an orchid flower when they wear it for decoration. They rarely realize that the flower is just waiting for some pollen.

One pollen grain is necessary for the development of every seed. Usually an orchid receives pollen in small masses, stuck together, for this is the way the pollen grains are freed from the stamen in another flower. A single flower may use nearly a million and a half pollen grains, for 1,450,000 seeds have been counted in a single orchid fruit.

Usually orchid seeds are barely bigger than a dust particle. They contain almost no store of food. If they are going to sprout, they must do so within less than a month from the time they are dispersed. If dry weather keeps an orchid seed from sprouting for a month, the seed dies. And even if it does sprout, the seedling cannot survive on its own. It cannot absorb the mineral substances it needs. A fungus partner must do this for it. To succeed, the seed must fall close to the right kind of fungus. Then an orchid plant can grow. Probably many kinds of orchids are rare because their seeds starve. They do not chance to fall beside the right fungus, or the weather is too dry for them to sprout.

One kind of orchid that is native to eastern Mexico is so important that people do not depend upon the right moth coming along with enough of the proper pollen. Instead, men and women gently transfer the pollen from the flowers of one plant to those of another. This plant is the vanilla orchid, the source of vanilla flavoring. Its seedlings take root in the soil and send up a long green stem as a vine. It clings to trees. The stem is fleshy, and as much as half an inch in diameter. Along the stem are shiny oval leaves 4 or 5 inches long. They clasp the stem at the one end, and narrow to a pointed tip at the other. So thick are the leaves that they scarcely show their veins.

Flower buds appear where the leaves of the vanilla orchid arise from the stem. Each bud becomes a side branch, displaying several creamy orchid flowers. From a distance insects see five petals radiating out like a star. At closer range they are attracted by a sixth petal. It is rolled up as a projecting tube much longer than the tubular part of a daffodil. Its orange lining is

epiphytic orchid

the target for insects that carry vanilla pollen. They go up the tubular petal for nectar, and inside exchange pollen from elsewhere for a new load.

The showy parts of the vanilla orchid eventually wither and disappear. All that is left is a fingerlike projection. It is the vanilla fruit. Generally it is known as a "vanilla bean," because of its shape and green color. Wild ones are usually less than 6 inches long and half an inch in diameter. Cultivated vanilla plants produce fruits almost twice this length.

The Indian people of Mexico and Central

Because of a Flower

America learned long ago how to extract vanilla flavoring from vanilla fruits. They willingly showed the painstaking process to the Spanish explorers. Essentially the same method is used today. The fruits are picked when they reach full size. Each morning the fruits are laid out on cloths to cure in the sun. Each afternoon they are taken indoors and covered with cloths "to sweat." At night they are enclosed in tight boxes as though they might get cold. In a month or so, the fruits darken and become flat, but shorten very little. A dark-colored resinous juice covers the whole fruit and makes it somewhat sticky. If the curing is done correctly and the fruits are of high quality, tiny crystals of vanillin form in the resin. They glisten in the sun, but are held firmly on the fruit. Pure vanilla extract is obtained from the cured beans by a special process. The vanillin crystals are dissolved and additional vanillin is recovered from the dark resinous juice. The extract is the delicious flavoring used in ice cream and cakes.

The Indians knew how to use vanilla flavoring in many ways. One way was to blend it with ground-up seeds from the strange fruits of a special kind of tree. The product was cocoa, which the Indians enjoyed drinking. The un-

The Extra-Special Orchids

usual tree is known today by its Spanish name *cacao* (pronounced kah-cow'). Its fruits resemble wrinkled melons, and the seeds inside the pulp are called "cocoa beans." The fruit hangs from the bark of the cacao tree because the flowers that produce the fruit appear there. They are visited by day by dung flies, which carry the cacao pollen. It seems strange that the two most favored flavorings in much of the world are chocolate made from ground-up cocoa beans and vanilla from the fruits of an orchid, and both are native to the Western Hemisphere. Today, the plants that produce these valuable substances are grown in many tropical countries far from their native lands. Foreign dung flies will serve the cacao flowers. But the vanilla flowers must be pollinated by human hands, because only the Mexican insects can do this work for the rewards the vanilla orchid offers.

In many of the Latin American countries, some native orchid of great beauty has been chosen for the national flower. The most modest of these is the dove flower or Holy Ghost orchid of Panama. Each white waxy blossom opens with others at the top of an upright stalk. At its center, around its stamen and pistil, is a

Because of a Flower

petal that resembles a white dove with wings upraised, behind a little pulpit.

Far more glamorous is the flower of the *Cattleya* orchid that has been selected as the emblem for Colombia, Costa Rica, and Guatemala. It too grows on an orchid plant that perches high up on the outstretched limb of a forest tree. But each blossom of a *Cattleya* has a lip in the form of a coiled tube, usually brightly colored inside where the stamen and pistil cling together. On each side of the tube are two wonderful flaring petals, sometimes measuring 6 inches across. Behind these are three lesser petals, one straight up, one downward to each side. They set off the showier parts of the orchid flower.

The flowers of most orchids retain their freshness for several days. In the wild, this ability to stay attractive is important for success in attracting insects with pollen. The lasting quality appeals to people in Hawaii and the South Pacific, who string together flowers of the smaller orchids to make garlands called leis. They are decorations to be worn around the neck, the head, or a hat, as tokens of welcome, affection, gratitude, or good-bye. In many other countries, a single large orchid flower is thought

The Extra-Special Orchids

of as a special gift, a token of esteem. It dominates a corsage and draws attention to the wearer.

At least 15,000 different kinds of orchids can be distinguished by examining their flowers. Together they make up the second largest family of flowering plants. Only the family to which the daisy and the dandelion belong has more members. The orchids attract animals to individual flowers, whereas the members of the daisy family attract insects to a number of flowers held close together in a flower head. The orchid flower and the animal that transports its pollen form a twosome. An orchid shows how far a plant can go in enhancing this one-to-one relationship.

The Flowers That Follow the Sun

> ". . the sunflower turns on her god, when he sets,
> The same look which she turn'd when he rose."
>
> —Thomas Moore (1780-1852)
> *Irish Melodies.* Believe Me,
> If All Those Endearing Young
> Charms, stanza 2.

EVERY FLOWER in a field of sunflowers faces the sun all day long. The flower petals themselves shine like golden rays of sunshine. Soon after dawn, every flower turns to the east. By noon it is facing the Equator. While the sun sets, the flower is facing west. The following day it renews its rhythm.

The sunflower makes its circuit following the sun once each 24 hours. You can almost see it turn if you watch early in the morning. It turns most quickly when the sun's rays first reach it. It turns because of differences in the rate of

common sunflower

growth between the side of the stalk where the sunshine falls and the side in the shade.

Every sunflower is more than one flower. It is hundreds of flowers in a compact group. All of them are attached to the end of the same stem. Only the outermost ring of flowers provide a showy display. Each of them has a single large, yellow petal. This glows in the sunlight and attracts insects to the flower head. All of the other flowers in the same head lack petals, but offer nectar and pollen. A bee can walk quickly over the tips of these petalless flowers, thrusting its "tongue" into one after another. This lets the petalless flowers collect pollen from the bees and produce seeds. The outer flowers are just for show.

The first petalless flowers to open in a sunflower head are the outer ones. Immediately, the petalless flowers nearest to them open too, and get ready to reward the bees and to benefit from the pollen they carry. Next a zone of flowers nearer the center becomes the attractive part of the head. By the time the centermost flowers have nectar and pollen to offer, the seeds are ripening just inside the outermost ring. Generally at this stage, the golden petals of the sunflower are battered and worn. They have held up for a

The Flowers That Follow the Sun

week or two regardless of what the weather may have been. Soon they wither and drop off. The parts on the petalless flowers that produced and caught the pollen shrivel and fall off, too. Now the pointed ends of all the seeds are suddenly in full view.

At the seed stage, the wonderful symmetry of the sunflower head shows more plainly than before. Each seed has an exact location. And every seed is flattened in such a way that one edge is toward the center of the head, the other toward the outside. This arrangement allows the seed to swell with stored food without causing the whole flower head to tear apart.

Today, sunflowers grow in many temperate countries. In none are they more appreciated by wildlife and by mankind than in their native North America. But no longer do the sunflowers spring up on the Great Plains the way they used to. Two hundred years ago, these plants had millions of prairie dogs and bison as animal neighbors. Wherever a prairie dog threw out earth while it was enlarging its underground burrow, sunflower seeds sprouted in the bare soil. The seedlings grew and blossomed and produced more seeds. The bison ate and trampled the prairie grasses, making places for sunflow-

Because of a Flower

ers to grow. When a bison lay down and rolled, to take a dust bath, it left bare soil. Sunflowers sprang up. The prairie dogs ate some of the sunflower seeds. Prairie chickens and meadowlarks ate even more. And Indian children scurried from one sunflower to another, to collect the fat seeds, each striped with gray.

From central Canada southward to Peru, the Indians regarded the sunflower as a sacred plant. It signified the sun, which gives energy to all life. The Indians carried sunflowers in their religious dances, and made sunflower designs a part of their handicrafts.

Today, the sunflowers grow even taller on the Great Plains. But the plants rise in solid stands behind high fences around large fields. Machinery is used to bare the soil where the sunflowers are to grow. Similar fields can be found in the USSR, India, Egypt, and Peru, to which sunflowers have been introduced. In some of these fields, the sunflowers tower more than 15 feet tall, with gigantic flower heads as much as 2 feet across. As soon as the seeds are ripe, the whole plant is harvested.

Some of the seeds are saved and planted so that there will be another crop next year. More of the sunflower seeds go into bags, to be sold

The Flowers That Follow the Sun

to people who wish to give them to wild birds or to indoor pets, such as parrots. Still more sunflower seeds are squeezed in special machines, to extract a valuable yellow oil that can be used in place of olive oil. Or it can be made into margarine or artist's paints. The residue from the squeezed seeds is called oil cake. It is given to poultry and livestock as a food supplement, particularly in Scandinavia. The sunflower stalks and leaves are saved, too. Although coarse, they are cut up and fed to livestock during the wintertime.

The sunflowers that wild animals enjoy are mostly wild plants. They grow in pastures and along roadsides. Some of them live only a single year. They grow tall, flower and produce seeds, then die before winter. Other kinds grow up again from roots that stay alive underground. One of these perennial sunflowers stores food in its roots, which become swollen and edible, almost like sweet potatoes. The plant is known as the Jerusalem artichoke. This name is a double mistake, based on a misunderstanding. It began in 1604, when the French explorer Samuel de Champlain arrived at Cape Cod. He saw the Indians of that part of Massachusetts eating a strange vegetable. He did not know that these natives had dug up sunflower roots and cooked them. Champlain and his men sampled some of the roots, both cooked and raw, and decided that they tasted most like artichokes. He took some live roots to Europe, where they were grown to show what peculiar plants lived in America.

The strange plants grew wonderfully well in Europe. Soon the people of Italy were raising them and calling them *girasole*, which means "turn with the sun." When the English got some plants of this kind from the Italians, they translated *girasole* as Jerusalem. The English also believed the roots to actually be artichokes —not just something that had a similar taste. The mistake has never been corrected. But the sunflowers called Jerusalem artichokes still grow wild along streams in loose moist soil, particularly in North America east of the Mississippi River. Their flowers keep turning to face the sun.

Any plant with flowers as large and bright as those of the sunflower is sure to attract animals. Countless insects visit the flower heads. Nor are bees the only ones to carry the pollen. Flesh flies, which ordinarily go to carrion, come to alight on the petalless flowers and sip the nec-

The Flowers That Follow the Sun

tar. Butterflies and day-flying moths pay frequent visits. Small beetles fold their hard wing covers and nibble at sunflower pollen. Each part of the country has a different assortment of insects that take advantage of the open sunflowers.

A very special butterfly comes to the golden sunflowers that grow close to woodlands, east of the Rockies and north of the Carolinas. It is the tawny-orange insect known as the silvery checkerspot because its underwings are almost silver white below. This checkerspot butterfly is numerous and familiar wherever the woodland sunflowers are common. But the butterfly is not often seen clearly for it is quick and elusive. It stays still the longest while it is laying an egg on a sunflower plant. Its brownish black caterpillars, which have an orange stripe along each side, eat sunflower leaves. Sometimes the full-grown caterpillars can be found in winter sleep under the sunflower plant among the dead leaves.

High above the ground, the sunflower heads attract goldfinches and chickadees. Like acrobats these little birds cling to the head. They peck at seeds that are getting ripe. Ripe ones are pulled out, one at a time. The bird shells the seed, and eats the contents. Blue jays work faster. They swallow the seeds whole, one after another until they can hold no more. A squirrel may climb the sturdy stalk of the sunflower to feast. Sometimes the squirrel uses its sharp front teeth to cut off the whole head, then finishes its meal seated on the ground. It drops many seeds. But mice and chipmunks find and eat almost every one.

Occasionally a sunflower head has no seeds to offer any of these animals. Tiny caterpillars of an inconspicuous moth have arrived before the seeds got ripe. Cutting into one seed after another, the caterpillars devoured everything inside. A few seeds will satisfy one small caterpillar. Yet a hundred of these insects can destroy every seed in a flower head.

The pattern of small flowers in a sunflower head is very much like the pattern in related flowers, the daisies. Daisies differ in facing upward, toward the sky, and in not following the sun. The daisy of early summer is the marguerite, which has a yellow center surrounded by white petals. The old game of "Loves me, loves me not," comes out happily only when the daisy has an odd number of petals, rather than an even one. Actually the plant is a wild chrysanthemum. It came to America from Eu-

The Flowers That Follow the Sun

rope and spread as a weed. Now the spicy odor from its finely divided leaves has contributed to the gentle fragrances of summer. The later daisies have coarser leaves and less perfume. They are bigger, with golden yellow petals and a cone-shaped brown center. Known as black-eyed Susans or coneflowers, they formerly lived from the Great Plains westward. Now they grow along roadsides and in vacant fields all the way to the Atlantic coast.

But in America, it is a native sunflower, rather than a daisy, that completes a summer.

The Yucca and Its Partners

> Friendly scarecrows,
> the Joshua trees
> stay dressed
> for Halloween.
>
> —Donald M. Murray

A CLUSTER of yucca flowers shows so conspicuously against the sky even at night, by starlight, that the Indians in the Southwest call the cluster a "candle of God." And this attractive plant is also honored in other ways. There is a town of Yucca in western Arizona, a Yucca Mountain in southern Nevada, and a village of Yucca near the Missouri River in North Dakota.

The word *yucca* comes from none of these places. It is a Haitian word, from the people of Haiti in the West Indies. Yuccas are native to

The Yucca and Its Partners

the sandy soils of the West Indies. They also grow naturally on the American continent in the eastern coastal states from North Carolina southward, around the Gulf of Mexico, and down into Mexico and Central America. Yuccas are at home too from the deserts of the Southwest all the way north into the Canadian prairies. In some of these places they are called soapweed, silk grass, or bear grass.

Usually a yucca plant shows no stem at all before it starts to flower. The roots come to an evergreen bud at ground level. This single bud produces narrow, pointed leaves, which project in all directions. On some yuccas the leaves are so stiff and sharp at the tip that the plant is known as Spanish bayonet, or Adam's needle. Lizards, insects, and other small animals find safety among the leaves. No bobcat or insect-eating bird risks being stuck by a leaf tip by trying to catch prey in these hiding places.

When the season is right, a yucca plant produces a tall, slender stem that is its flower stalk. You can almost see it grow, for every day it is several inches taller than it was the day before. It grows to be 8 to 15 feet tall while short side branches produce the flower buds. The flowers open in a great cluster, sometimes a foot in di-

Because of a Flower

ameter and 4 feet high from bottom to top. Each flower in the cluster is waxy white, or slightly greenish, or a pale creamy color.

Every flower of a yucca resembles a white tulip flower. It has six petals, which spread apart to reveal six stamens and a central pistil. These features show that the plant belongs to the lily family.

For more than a hundred years after yuccas were discovered in America, no scientist noticed anything really special about a yucca flower. Yet there is something strange. The pollen that the stamens produce is always stuck together, as though it had been mixed with honey. No insect can accidentally brush against a stamen and get dusted with yucca pollen. A tiny insect may even get its feet stuck in the sticky material.

The secret of the yucca flower is unlocked by only one type of small silvery moth. These moths begin to fly around and find mates at the season when the yucca flowers are starting to open. A moth that has eggs ready to be laid will fly at night to an open yucca flower. First, she creeps over a stamen and examines the pollen, as though to be sure it has the right consistency. Next, she uses special projecting parts on either side of her mouth to pick out and form some of

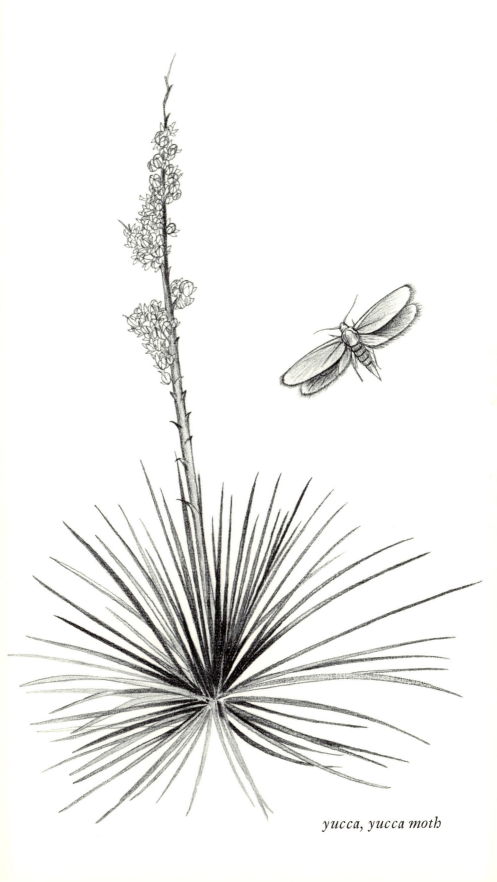

yucca, yucca moth

the pollen into a ball bigger than her head. Now, she spreads her wings and flies to another open yucca flower, still carrying the ball of pollen. This time, she stabs a few of her eggs into the lower part of the pistil. Afterward she carefully stuffs pollen from her sticky ball into little cup-shaped cavities at the top of the pistil. Finally, she creeps to a stamen and there gets a new ball of pollen. With it she flies to still another yucca flower to repeat the process. She continues until she has placed all her eggs, or can find no more open yucca flowers.

Without guidance, the moth puts the pollen in exactly the right place to be useful to the yucca plant. The pollen enables the plant to begin producing about 200 seeds. But the seeds are only partly grown when the eggs of the moth hatch. Out come four or five little caterpillars. Each caterpillar eats its way to where the green seeds are and devours fewer than twenty of them. Rarely are there enough caterpillars to destroy even half of the seeds the yucca plant is producing. The rest of the seeds are likely to ripen.

In parts of the world where yucca plants have been introduced without their moths, not a single seed develops. The yucca flowers wither and

The Yucca and Its Partners

fall off without producing a pod or doing the plant any good. Yet the caterpillars of the moth are as dependent upon yucca plants as the yuccas are upon the moths. Without plenty of yuccas, these special insects have no future. As adult moths they cannot find places to lay eggs where the caterpillars will emerge in safety and find something good to eat. No moths of this type live where yuccas are uncommon.

The moth is a specialist, and so is the plant. They part company when the yucca pods swell around the ripening seeds. Then a small, round hole appears in each pod. The hole is cut by the caterpillars after they are full grown and ready to escape. They crawl out of the pod and let themselves down to the ground on strands of silk. Then each caterpillar uses its six short legs, which are near its head, and burrows into the earth.

A few inches below the surface, the caterpillar rests and then sheds its skin, as though it were a dress with a zipper down the back. Without the skin, the caterpillar becomes a pupa. Its body covering now resembles plates of armor with many stiff bristles on the outside, all pointing away from the head end. Within the bristly armor of the pupa, the insect slowly transforms

Because of a Flower

into a moth. The change will be complete by the time the yuccas are ready to flower again. Then the insect uses the stiff bristles on the pupa to help it creep out of the earth. Once in the open, the pupal armor splits apart. The moth escapes. It spreads its wings, covered with silvery scales, until they measure more than an inch from tip to tip. Those wings will carry the moth on its first flight, to find a mate and a yucca flower.

The partnership between the yucca plant and the moths that carry its pollen is only the beginning of the story, however. Animals of many other kinds turn up to share in the benefits of the relationship. Some seem designed merely to distract attention from the silvery moths that perform the magic of pollination. There are several kinds of moths always found nearby that have ash gray wings or spotted ones. Known as "bogus yucca moths," they are smaller members of the same big family as the moths that carry the yucca pollen. But they have no special projecting parts at each side of the mouth with which to gather sticky pollen into a ball. This does not prevent the bogus yucca moths from coming to yucca flowers that their cousins have already pollinated. These unproductive indi-

The Yucca and Its Partners

viduals show little interest in an open blossom. They come, instead, to a branch supporting a flower that has already closed. Or they come to the swelling pistil of a flower that has already dropped its petals and stamens. There the bogus yucca moths mate and lay a few eggs. Their caterpillars emerge and feed on the side branch or on the enlarging pod. Neither of these green parts would be available as food if the true yucca moths had not brought pollen to the flower.

There is good reason for the bogus yucca moths being smaller than those that transfer the yucca pollen. Their caterpillars get less nutritious food and take only a little of it to complete their growth. Long before the yucca seeds ripen or the pod dries, getting ready to drop from the plant, these smaller caterpillars move to the ground. There they find a safe place in which to spin a cocoon. It would be harmful to the future of the bogus yucca moths if their caterpillars interfered with the success of either the yucca plant or the true yucca moths that carry yucca pollen.

Much larger insects also take advantage of the abundant yucca plants in the American Southwest and Mexico. They are the giant skipper butterflies, which are found nowhere else in the

Because of a Flower

world. These butterflies fly with unusual speed on their brown wings that are 2 to 3 inches across. But they stay away from the yucca flowers, the pods, and the seeds. A female giant skipper with eggs to lay darts directly to the bottom of the tall, upright stalk that holds the cluster of yucca flowers. She folds her wings together vertically above her back while she attaches a single egg near the ground. When the caterpillar hatches, it eats a passageway into the yucca stalk. Then it has a choice. It may extend its tunnel upward, eating out the pith at the center of the stalk. This hollows out the stalk just as a person might to make a whistle. Later anyone can cut off the hollow stalk above and below the entrance hole and blow through it. Or the caterpillar can turn downward, to feed inside the roots of the yucca. Whichever way it goes, the caterpillar soon returns to its entrance hole and begins to spin a long silken tube. This will be a container for its wastes. Afterward, when the caterpillar is full grown, it will use the silken tube as a place in which to transform into a butterfly. Then the tube becomes a shelter, a place where the insect is invisible, and no bird or lizard will attack it. Often a search reveals one of these tubes far in among the yucca leaves.

The Yucca and Its Partners

Many birds and lizards do come to yucca plants to hunt for food. Small birds and mice come also to tear off loose fibers that project as wisps and curls along the sides of yucca leaves. These fibers make a soft lining for a nest. The Indians in yucca country obtain longer, stronger fibers from the whole leaves. The Indian uses a knife to cut off a few leaves, and then pounds them between two stones. The green part of the leaf can then be scraped away, exposing the white fibers inside. The Indian combs the fibers to separate them, and hangs them to dry in the sun. These shiny fibers are called "istle" by the Indians. They can be used to make coarse cloth for bags, and also to make rope.

A yucca plant produces many new leaves each year. From its root it also sends out side shoots, and these grow upward with new buds and more leaves. Each bud usually sends out a tall stalk with flowers in spring. If the weather brings rain in late summer, the yucca may produce a second cluster of flowers at that time. But whether it blooms once or twice, with the help of its moth partners, a yucca spills out thousands of seeds from its pods each year. Only a few of these seeds are needed to produce new yucca plants when the old one dies. The rest of the seeds provide food for animals in yucca country.

The antelope ground squirrels of the deserts in the American Southwest and Mexico rely upon finding plenty of yucca seeds when cactus seeds are scarce. But finding yucca seeds is not easy. Yucca seeds are flat and lie close to the sandy soil. The black color of the seed makes it resemble a shadow, perhaps a small, round hole in the soil like the opening of an ant nest. A squirrel must hop over the ground, examining every small, dark spot, to find yucca seeds. If the desert has too few seeds of this kind, the squirrel goes hungry. Or it goes elsewhere.

Some yuccas grow to tree size in California near Mexico, and in Mexico itself. They have woody trunks, which branch grotesquely to a height of about 30 feet. At the end of each branch is a bud. It produces many leaves, and also a cluster of flowers in season. Early explorers who crossed the deserts, where no trees grow, thought they were coming to better land when they saw these strange yucca trees. Surely, they thought, water and food must be only a short distance ahead. And so they pressed on and discovered the Pacific coast. When they told about their escape from the hardships of

The Yucca and Its Partners

the desert, they remembered the yucca trees that seemed to point the way. It was like the biblical story of Joshua, who succeeded Moses and led the Children of Israel out of the deserts into the Promised Land. The yucca trees became known as Joshua trees.

A yucca of any kind in flower gives beauty and encouragement wherever it grows. It offers food and fiber. And it shows how perfect a partnership a plant may have with an animal, even if it is only a silvery moth. Yet this wonderful cooperation limits the yucca, too. The plant can produce seeds only where the right kind of moths are common. If you try to cultivate a yucca beyond the area of the Americas where yucca moths live, the plant produces flowers year after year. But it remains a stranger, unfruitful in its new environment. More than most plants, it shows how important familiar neighbors are.

The Flowering Oak Tree

How do you tell how much rain the summer will bring? Watch the tree flowers!

If the Oak's before the Ash,
Then you'll only get a splash;
If the Ash before the Oak,
Then you may expect a soak.

—Old English proverb.

THOUGH MANY PLANTS depend on animals to deliver their pollen from flower to flower, not all do. Animals are of no help to an oak tree until its acorns are ripe. But oak trees help animals every month of the year.

For about a week each spring, an oak tree is in flower. It produces stamens and pollen in one type of flower and a pistil and later acorns in another. The buds that conceal the flowers with pollen grow very quickly. In only a day or two they appear and are ready to open. They suddenly hang downward below the branches, in

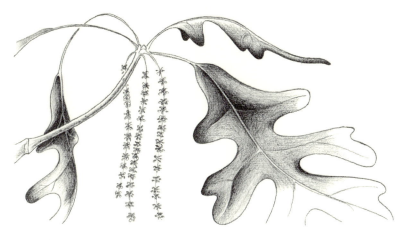

oak flowers

greenish yellow clusters like limp braids of hair. The individual flowers are barely an eighth of an inch across. They have no petals to hide the short stamens, which number from four to eight. The clusters swing gently in every breeze and shake into every passing breeze a mist of microscopic pollen grains. The wind carries the pollen from one tree to the next, so long as the oaks grow reasonably close together.

The tree sheds these pendant flowers as soon as the pollen is gone. The clusters tumble to the ground. Soon they are dry and brittle. They break into fragments and are seen no more. Their work is done.

During the week that the wind is carrying the oak pollen from tree to tree, the second group of oak flowers is also open. These are close to the branches, on short side spurs. Not one of them has a petal. Instead, a little cup composed of overlapping scales surrounds a central, solitary pistil. At first the tip of the pistil projects in three directions at once, and each projection is sticky. Pollen from the wind adheres to the sticky material. Afterward, the tip of the pistil shrivels and turns black, as the fertilized pistil creates a seed with a heavy outer coating—an acorn. Often the pistil tip remains on the tip of the acorn, even after the acorn grows to full size and drops off the tree. Seldom does anyone notice.

The flowering of each oak tree occurs while its new leaves are small. The tree has not yet offered much shade from the noonday sun. Around its base the spring wildflowers may be in full bloom. Their display ceases when the oak leaves expand and overlap. They shield the woodland soil from the sun and interfere with the flow of air. The tree could not rely on breezes to transport pollen at this stage. Nor are there breezes to carry away the moisture that the forest creatures need. The woodland soil under oak trees remains humid all summer. The dense shade stays cool.

In the southern part of the United States, trees known as live oaks also produce their flow-

The Flowering Oak Tree

ers early in the year. Live oaks are evergreen because their old leaves stay green all winter. Their leaves are small, and let the wind blow through.

Each kind of oak tree follows its own pattern in producing flowers and acorns. But by examining the pistil or the ripe acorn of any kind of oak, you can tell what kind of tree it is. The shape of the leaf and the nature of the bark also say that a tree is an oak. But oak trees do differ. If it is a white oak, a chestnut oak, or a live oak, the projecting points from the pistil will be extremely short. The acorn will ripen by autumn and be ready to sprout at once. The cup that holds the acorn is thick and corky. The shell of the acorn itself is smooth on the inside, and the kernel of the nut is likely to be sweet, not bitter. These are the acorns the Indians preferred. They gathered great quantities, dried and ground the kernels, and made the flour into bread. The leaves of these oaks have smoothly rounded lobes, while the leaves of some oaks have sharp points. You can tell the difference even with your eyes closed, simply by feeling the leaves. You can also feel the difference between oaks by touching the bark. Some is smooth, but some is scaly, and remains pale

Because of a Flower

brownish gray into old age. The English oak, which grows over much of Europe, follows this tradition. It is a famous tree because its wood is so hard and strong, suitable for making wooden ships and fine furniture.

A red oak or a black oak starts out very differently from the oaks above. In the flower that will produce an acorn, the tip of the pistil extends in three threadlike projections. The acorn needs nearly a year and a half to ripen. It drops to the ground the second autumn, and will not sprout until the following spring. The cup that holds the acorn is formed of thin scales. Inside, the shell of the acorn is hairy, and the kernel of the nut has a bitter taste. The Indians had to extract the bitterness before making bread from acorns of these kinds. The bitter substance comes out if the acorn kernels are soaked or boiled in water, then dried in the sun. The leaves of these oaks feel sharp. The edges have bristly points. Actually the veins extend a short distance beyond the blade. And the bark is leathery, rather than scaly. It retains some green color until it blackens.

Most of the animals that benefit from oak trees show little preference as to kind. They come quietly, inconspicuously, to browse on

The Flowering Oak Tree

oak seedlings or to eat the acorns. Deer and wild hogs gobble up whatever they can. One wild turkey that was shot had seventy-seven black oak acorns in its crop. Another had thirty-five of the much larger acorns dropped by a northern red oak. Black bear and squirrels fatten on acorns before winter comes. No other flowering tree in the United States provides so much bounty each year for mammals and birds.

Squirrels are most often seen scampering up and down an oak tree. They and oaks go together for a good reason. Most oak trees grow from an acorn that a squirrel has buried and failed to dig up later. The squirrel caches vast numbers of them. It digs a hole with its forepaws, drops in the acorn it has been carrying in its mouth, pulls soil into the hole, and tamps down the surface. Probably a squirrel relies less on memory than on a keen sense of smell to find the acorn again. Often a buried acorn is dug up and eaten by a squirrel other than the one that buried it. But enough acorns remain to keep oak trees flowering in the forest.

In early summer the squirrels cut off leafy branches from oak trees. They push the branches together to build a shelter in a crotch high above the ground. The squirrels spend each

Because of a Flower

night in these shelters and hide their babies there. The untidy summer house may not be noticeable until after most of the leaves drop from the oak in autumn. By then the squirrels have moved out into warmer quarters, such as a big knothole, for the cold months ahead.

Squirrels sometimes help oak trees unwittingly, in an unexpected way. A squirrel kills and eats many insects that destroy acorns. One squirrel may spend a half-hour at a time sorting through the acorns below an oak. It picks up and drops every acorn that could sprout and produce a new tree. But it bites into each acorn that conceals a beetle larva. These acorns must have a different smell. Using its sharp front teeth, the squirrel cuts through the shell and the kernel to reach the larva. Neatly it picks out the insect and devours it, then goes hunting for another. By opening every "bad" acorn and discarding all the "good" ones, the squirrel diminishes the number of beetle larvae that will reach maturity.

The beetle itself is an acorn weevil, and a truly amazing insect. Its pale brown body is egg-shaped, about a quarter of an inch in length. At the head end it has a slender beak as long as the rest of its body or, in some females, as much as

acorn weevil   *oak gall, gall wasp*

twice as long! With this extraordinary beak, the female beetle bores a small hole through the shell of an acorn that is not yet ripe. She lays an egg in the hole, and may close the opening with a bit of excrement. Usually this plug turns white and marks the spot where the egg was laid. Meanwhile, inside, the egg hatches. The larva begins to eat. It destroys the acorn before emerging to transform into an adult beetle. There would be many more of these insects if squirrels did not seek them out as an attractive change in diet.

Birds that eat insects often patrol the leaves and bark of oak trees to find their favorite foods. Warblers and orioles inspect the top and bottom of each leaf. Brown creepers and nuthatches climb up and down the tree trunks, peering and poking into crevices of the bark where insects

Because of a Flower

hide. Chickadees cling to rough bark and twigs, searching for tidbits to eat. And if any insect takes to its wings, trying to fly to another tree, a flycatcher bird such as a wood pewee is likely to pursue and eat it. Even among the fallen leaves at the base of the oak tree an insect is not safe. A thrush may turn the leaf over and find the insect. Or a tiny furry shrew, far smaller than a mouse, will be scrambling among the leaves following insects wherever they go on the ground.

A good many insects succeed in laying eggs on oak flowers, or on leaves or bark, before getting caught. Immature insects hatch out and conceal themselves someplace on the tree where they can get nourishment. The young of various beetles use their strong jaws to cut tunnels, some in the inner bark, some in the hard wood of the oak. They go in so far that only a big woodpecker can peck its way to where they live and eat.

A few of these immature beetles grow to be almost 2 inches long. They can barely squeeze through tunnels more than a quarter of an inch in diameter. When they chew on the wood, it vibrates. A person can hear the vibrations by pressing one ear against the bark. *Crunnnch!*

The Flowering Oak Tree

Later these insects mature and emerge into the forest. Some of them have very long feelers and are called longicorn beetles. Others have flattened oval bodies that shine in the sun as though they were made of metal. They are metallic wood borers.

Still other insects live in knotholes or in places where the bark is coming loose on a dead branch. They feed on fungi that attack dead wood, or they prey on smaller insects that eat the fungi. A single oak tree may have dozens of different insects living inside it. But the oak is there only because an earlier tree had flowers that produced an acorn.

About 300 different kinds of minute animals induce oaks to provide them with a special home as well as food. A few of these animals are spider mites. The rest are aphids, tiny moths, gall midges and gall wasps. They produce chemical substances that induce the tree to grow abnormally. It forms a hollow bulge, with the gall maker at the center. The bulge is the gall. Its shape gives a reliable clue to the kind of animal inside. The most obvious ones on oaks are small projections above and below the leaves, or on the stems. One tiny gall wasp causes a spherical gall the size of a Ping-Pong ball on a leaf. Inside the smooth tan skin are strong fibers that radiate from the chamber at the center, where the immature gall wasp lives. A different gall wasp causes oaks in Asia Minor to produce vast numbers of hard galls that have a commercial value. They are rich in tannic and gallic acids, which are useful in tanning leather and in making inks of outstanding permanence. An extract from the Aleppo gall on Syrian oaks has contributed to the lasting quality of important documents for more than a thousand years. The legal, literary, and educational professions depend on this material. Gall extract is specified in the formulas for inks used by the United States Treasury, the Bank of England, the German Chancellery, and the Danish government, to name a few. Yet nobody gives much thought to the insects that sting the oak into forming the distinctive galls. The insects are forgotten, just as are the inconspicuous flowers that start the life of each new oak.

Oak leaves contain tannic acid, too. It makes them resist the action of bacteria and as a result they are slow to disintegrate once they fall to the ground. The tannic acid from the leaves increases the acidity of the soil in an oak forest. This, in turn, affects the sprouting of seeds. It

The Flowering Oak Tree

makes the soil favorable for oak seedlings and less suitable for those of many other trees. Consequently, oaks tend to segregate themselves into communities, with each oak reasonably close to another of the same kind. This is one of the reasons oaks can rely on the wind, instead of insects, to distribute their pollen in spring.

Man has long admired the oak tree. Oaks still provide more hardwood for construction than any other flowering plant in the forest. And it is not man alone who uses oaks for building. Beaver cut down oak trees that grow near a beaver pond. They eat the leathery, dark green bark of black oaks and red oaks. And they build the strong branches into beaver dams and beaver lodges.

Oaks that are not cut down by man or beaver, or are not otherwise destroyed, grow old. Some live nearly 200 years. By then they are huge trees and have lost many big branches. Often a knothole, where a branch broke off, provides a home for some animal. If the hole is small, it will perhaps shelter a chickadee. If it is larger, it may be occupied by a family of screech owls. The oldest wood at the center of the oak is likely to rot and provide a bigger cavity. It might suit a family of opossums or raccoons. A really big hollow oak with a spacious doorway becomes a den for a bear.

Eventually the old oak can no longer resist the weight of ice in winter and the gales of March. It tumbles to the ground and becomes the home of animals that find shelter or food in fallen logs. Mosses grow over the old tree. It melts into the soil. But oaks nearby are flowering inconspicuously every spring. One of them provides the acorn that will sprout right where the old oak fell. Up grows a new oak seedling. It, too, can rise to become a towering, flowering oak.

Cactus Flower

> The cactus
> squats on its round bottom,
> smug, green,
> in all that desert brown.
>
> —Donald M. Murray

A CACTUS is an American achievement in the flowering world. It is a plant that excels in surviving where two or three years may pass between one rain and the next. Most cacti live in deserts where the sun beats down every day from a cloudless sky. Every night the desert soil cools off, only to be reheated soon after dawn. Cacti of all sizes wait through the heat and cold for the rain to come. When they do, the plants grow a little and display their handsome flowers. Although the plant itself generally has a strange shape, the blossoms seem to be the

Because of a Flower

roses of the desert.

Even where rain comes more frequently and the air is not so dry as in a desert, you can find cacti. Usually they have no leaves, only thick stems, covered by a waterproof skin, that guard a store of water. The outside of the stems are studded with spines and little circles of barbed prickles. No other plants are protected in this way.

You can easily walk into a clump of cacti on any sandy ground. The early explorers who came to America did so when their ships landed. In the East, the men found these spiny plants from Massachusetts southward all the way to Argentina. On the Pacific coast, the colonists encountered cacti from Chile north to Vancouver Island.

Although prickly plants of this type were unknown in the Old World, they are widespread in the Americas. They are native flowers in five provinces of Canada, and in all of the United States except northernmost New England. In the humid tropics, cacti find well-drained places to grow high up on branches of forest trees. The familiar Christmas cactus (and also the Easter cactus) are native to the rain forests of Brazil. These plants are named because, even far from home, they regularly produce flowers

Cactus Flower

at these holiday seasons. Christmas cactus and Easter cactus are unusual because they have no sharp spines or prickles.

The name *cactus* was in use in Europe before any of the plants were ever seen by a European. The Greeks called any prickly plant a *kaktos*. The Romans spelled it *cactus*, plural *cacti*. But the word was not limited to any particular kind of plant until what we call cactus plants, today, were brought from America. They seemed to need the name "cactus" more than any other type of prickly plant on earth; so now cactus does mean a specific kind of plant.

The cactus you are most likely to meet is the prickly pear. It is a particularly widespread and common type. In most areas of the United States, the plants sprawl over the ground and remain inconspicuous when not in flower. Often grasses and low shrubby plants almost hide these cacti. In the deserts, however, some prickly pears grow to be 5 feet tall. On the Galápagos Islands, in the Pacific Ocean west of Ecuador, they attain tree size. This means that most of their jointed stems are beyond reach of the giant tortoises, which eat them.

The "pears" are the red, ripe fruits that come after the flowers have appeared, along the

Because of a Flower

edges of the flattened segments of the jointed, branching stem. The fruits are sweet and safe to eat once the prickles are removed. The pack rats of the desert carefully take hold of one end of a fallen prickly pear fruit. They drag it over the ground, wearing off its prickles. A pack rat hoards dozens of these fruits for food. It eats the soft pulp and discards the small, hard seeds. Generally the pack rat hauls pieces of cactus stem, too, and builds a fortress of them over its hoard of fruit. No fox, bobcat, or great horned owl will pursue a pack rat into a pile of cactus pieces. But a badger or a slender snake may do so and frighten the rat into leaving by the back door, perhaps right into the mouth of a coyote that is waiting there.

The green segments of the prickly pear cactus are all parts of the branching stem, but they act like leaves. They capture energy from sunlight and carbon dioxide from the air. They make food for the plant and store it, along with moisture, inside the prickly skin.

The prickly pear, like most cacti, has just two real leaves during its whole lifetime. These two appear when the seed first sprouts. Ordinarily this happens right after a rainstorm. As soon as the soil dries out completely, the seedling drops

prickly pear

its leaves. From that time on, it grows simply by enlarging its green stem whenever it has more water. It can conserve its moisture for a longer time in this way, and survive the lasting droughts of desert country.

Each time a prickly pear is rained on, it is likely to grow a new extension or two on its stem. You can tell where each new growth began and ended because the stem is constricted at both places. As a result the stem seems to consist of segments jointed together. One constriction shows where the stem segment started to grow. The next constriction is where it stopped when the plant had no more water to spare for enlarging itself.

On many prickly pears, the segments of the stem are fairly flat on both sides and rounded along the rim. One type has stem segments the size and shape of a beaver's tail, and is called the "beaver-tail cactus." Buds appear along the rim of the youngest segments. Some of these are flower buds. Generally the plant opens these first. Its fruits may be ripening while the stem is still adding new segments from slightly different buds.

The segments of a different kind of prickly pear cactus look more like sausages. These stems

Cactus Flower

are cylindrical between constrictions. Plants of this type occur in the American Southwest and Latin America and are called by a Spanish name, *chollas* (pronounced choy′-yahs). Most of them are exceedingly spiny. Long sharp needles stick out straight in all directions from each stem segment. Around the base of each needle are dozens of short, stiff bristles, every one of them barbed along its sides.

The youngest segments of a cholla stem have two special abilities: they can produce flowers and fruits; and they can snap off of the older parts of the cholla. Often this happens when a deer or other large animal blunders into a cholla cactus, either in the dark of night or while running carelessly by day. The sharp spines jab into the animal's skin. The whole segment breaks off and is carried away, stuck to the animal. It all happens so quickly that people who live in the desert often claim that the stem segments jump off the plant and stick to any passerby. For that reason these plants are often called "jumping chollas." By the time the animal shakes off the stem segment, the piece is some distance from the plant on which it grew. If a pack rat does not drag it away as building material for a fortress, the cholla segment may

Because of a Flower

take root after the next rain. It has become a separate plant.

Chollas with long sharp spines are fearsome plants. Yet the cactus wren can alight on a spine. The bird dodges the armament and carries nest material far in among the older segments of the branching stem. There a family of young wrens will be snug and reasonably safe. Unless a snake risks being stuck by the short stiff bristles around each spine of a cholla, it is unlikely to slither up the cactus and eat the young birds. Some people with a strange sense of humor collect the cholla bristles and grind them up to make "itch powder." More frequently the Indians who live where chollas grow gather the ripe "pears" to peel and eat.

When any kind of prickly pear is old enough and has had enough rain to produce flowers, it wastes no time. In less than a week its flower buds appear and enlarge on the youngest segments of stems. The green scales that overlap, protecting each flower, curl out of the way. The showy parts, which all appear to be petals, may be white, red, orange, or yellow. A few kinds of cactus have green flowers and are inconspicuous to our eyes. But the green flowers reflect the ultraviolet rays of sunlight, which insects see although we cannot. The insects find the green "ultraviolet flowers" extremely attractive, and go from one to the next with pollen.

A cactus flower has no prickles. The flower is there to attract animals, not to repel them. Each flower of a prickly pear resembles a single rose with many thin petals. They form a saucer behind a large number of golden stamens and a central pistil.

As soon as the flower opens, an amazing number of different animals arrive! By night, moths come on softly whirring wings. Each moth hovers while it uncoils its long tongue and probes below the stamens for a sip of nectar. Then it recoils its tongue like a watch spring and moves to another flower. By day the visitors are flies and bees, beetles and an occasional butterfly. Hummingbirds come at dawn and again before evening twilight. Larger birds perch wherever they can, hoping to catch some insects. Sometimes a bobcat or a coyote tries to make a sneak attack, to capture one of the larger birds.

More animals are active on a desert when the cacti are in flower than at any other time. Ordinarily these creatures hide from the heat of day. Their habits change after a good rain. Rain

Because of a Flower

synchronizes the events in the desert. The plants wait until the rain comes. As soon as moisture reaches their roots, their flower buds begin to expand. The rain seeps through the soil to insects that await this signal. Some insects are already mature. They climb upward into the daylight. Other insects are still doll-like, in their pupal armor; but as soon as they feel moisture, they emerge as adults.

By the time the flowers are ready to offer food to insects, insects are there to visit the flowers. Spadefoot toads appear from their deep hiding places, to dine on the insects. Birds fly in to look for insects. When birds see a dark storm cloud at a great distance, they fly for miles to reach the area of desert on which the clouds drop their torrent of rain. Some instinct tells them that that is where the plants will soon blossom, and the insects will begin flying from one flower to the next.

White-winged doves fly farther than any other birds to visit an area of cactus flowers. They come to the tallest of the cacti, the grotesque saguaro cacti of southern Arizona and northern Mexico. They may be as much as 50 feet tall, with twisted armlike branches. The doves migrate out of Latin America to visit

Cactus Flower

saguaro flowers. Each large saguaro stem or branch bears a high crown of firm white flowers. Gently the birds settle on the flowers and dip into one after another for sweet liquid. As they bend, the doves brush their soft breast feathers against the blossoms and transfer the pollen the cactus flowers produce. Insects are much less important in pollination of these flowers than the birds. But the doves are back in Mexico, or farther away than that by the time the saguaro fruits are ripe.

The people of Arizona have chosen the saguaro flower as their state emblem. Their finest stand of these special plants has been set aside as a national monument. In this protected area, some of the saguaros are believed to be 200 years old. A big one may weigh 30 tons after a period of rainy weather, when it is full of moisture. Its stem is pleated vertically and expands like an accordion to hold the water. These cacti produce an abundance of flowers and fruits, each fruit containing about 200 seeds. Yet almost every seed is eaten by some animal. Scientists have discovered that the only way the seeds of saguaros have a chance of surviving and sprouting today is for someone to take them and cover them with a screened cage. If the animals are kept out, the seeds sprout and the young plants grow. They need ten years to attain a height of 1 foot. Until then their armaments of spines are not strong enough to protect them.

The small rodents that eat saguaro seeds and the jackrabbits that eat young seedlings are far more numerous than they used to be. No longer are their numbers kept down by bobcats, coyotes, golden eagles, and great-horned owls. These predatory animals have been trapped and hunted in the surrounding desert to make it safe for livestock. And indirectly this program interferes with the future of the giant cacti, and of lesser cacti as well.

Under the best conditions, each cactus flower lasts only two or three days. The fruits and seeds that follow make the dry lands habitable for many animals. Yet a continuing succession of young plants growing big enough to flower is needed too. Cacti must survive if the entire community of life is to survive. They are important among the small number of special plants that can survive long periods of drought. Their nearest neighbors are mostly grasses in the prairies and along sandy coasts, and in a desert, shrubs with leathery leaves, such as the creosote bush, or trees with tremendously deep roots

blacktail jackrabbit

Because of a Flower

such as the cottonwood. On the stony, high ground in Colorado you will find cacti under scattered pines amid paintbrush and purple lupines. In all of these communities, the cacti provide a sudden splendor as they blossom forth in myriad colors after a spring rain.

The Many Heads of the Foxtail Grasses

> When earth is cut,
> grass heals the wound.
>
> —Donald M. Murray

WOULD YOU ever suspect that a lowly grass is a flowering plant, or one with an enchanted life? Yet it takes only a moment's thought to realize that grass can survive almost any catastrophe. Its leaves can be bitten off; they grow again immediately. Snow and ice cause no important damage to grass. Some grass needs no water for most of the year. A raging fire can burn it to the ground and cause no lasting damage. When green, the grass bends with the wind, rippling like waves in the sea. Green or dry, the grass sustains vast herds of grazing animals and

Because of a Flower

countless lesser kinds as well; and unless it is overgrazed, it goes on growing. Without thinking, we step on these plants and yet expect them to stay green.

Grasses provide all of our grain, corn, and rice. They nourish more people in temperate lands than all other flowering plants put together. Yet seldom does anyone notice when most grasses come into flower.

Grasses are suited magnificently for life on the windswept plains. They spread into these lands about 60 million years ago. Prior to that, the plains had no flowering plants of any kind. Today, grasslands occupy about a third of all the habitable territory on earth. Above ground the narrow leaves catch the sunlight. Underground, the fibrous roots interlace. They form a turf that resists erosion by wind or water. The grasses store nourishment in their roots and in stems that stretch out horizontally over the surface of the ground. In both places the stored foods are out of harm's way. Yet the grass can use them quickly for branching of the stems and for upward extension of leaves to capture energy from the sun.

The various grasses take turns in producing clusters of miniature flowers of exquisite perfec-

foxtail grass

tion. You can see these displays early in the growing season on some grasses, and later in others. Each kind of grass arranges its flowers in a different way on special flowering branches. From the arrangement, rather than from the delicate parts of the flowers themselves, you can tell which grass is which. Fortunately, the dozens of flowers in each flower head give the whole head a characteristic shape and color. The common grasses can be recognized by their heads, even from a distance.

Because of a Flower

To see clearly how an individual grass flower opens, you must look at it through a magnifying lens. The details are more refined than the mechanism in the smallest lady's wristwatch. They adjust themselves to both the rising of the sun and to the humidity. On a cloudy morning, or if the humidity is very high, the flower stays shut. Two pointed, spoon-shaped scales seal in all of the important parts. These include a central pistil with a pointed tip, three stamens, and two small knobs that are the closest thing to a petal that any grass flower contains.

Nobody knows yet where the grass plant conceals a clock, a weather station, and a communications network. Yet it opens its flowers as though it possessed all of these. On a suitable morning, at the appropriate hour, the two small knobs begin to swell inside each flower that is due to open. The knobs act as levers. They swing the spoon-shaped scales wide apart as smoothly as if they were doors operated by electric motors. Another pressure mechanism then causes the three stamens to emerge from hiding. Their thread-thin stalks raise up the slender pollen sac at the tip of each, and turn it outward into full view. In an hour or less, the pollen sacs split lengthwise and shake a dust of golden pollen into the passing air. Soon the sacs are empty, and the stamens wilt. The grass flower has done half its job.

Next the pointed tip of the pistil separates into three parts. Each part expands into a feathery trap for pollen. Until noon the flower may stay open, catching whatever pollen it can from the wind. By noon on a warm, dry day, the flower is likely to close again, its tasks fulfilled. Other flowers in the same grass head will repeat the process the following morning.

The air has a fragrant freshness during the hours when the grasses shed their shining pollen grains and let them drift away in whatever direction the breeze blows. The same moving air is picking up moisture from dewdrops on grassblades and spider webs. It is carrying perfume to summon bees to flowers of other kinds.

The grasses need no bees. Grasses ordinarily live in open country and so close together that air movements transfer their pollen efficiently. Seldom does a pistil in a head of grass flowers fail to receive the pollen it requires to set its seed. Each grass head matures into many of these hard, starch-filled fruits. Every one of them is a nutritious grain. Often it is still protected by the spoon-shaped scales that spread open and closed again on the day when the flower appeared. They are the "chaff" that must be loosened by threshing and removed in preparing grains for human use.

On many grasses, one of the scales around each fruit extends outward as a long bristle. The many bristles on each head often help us recognize the grass. Those on wild oats, for example, are rough and twisted. They catch easily on the fur of a passing animal and yank the seed so hard that it breaks from the plant and is carried along like a burr. On rye and wheat, the bristles are smooth and curve only slightly. But they are very long. Those of rye grass stick out stiffly at an angle on two sides of the head. Those of wheat arise all around the head and follow its contour.

The bristles on the head of foxtail grass are so long and silky, projecting on all sides but curving toward the end of the head, that the head does resemble a fox's tail. Those on the giant foxtail grass conceal the ripe seeds in a head that may be a foot long, 2 to 3 inches in diameter, and wave as much as 12 feet above the marshy ground. In winter these heads turn straw-yellow and yield their fruits to birds that come to peck at them. The giant foxtails are

The Many Heads of the Foxtail Grasses

native to brackish swales from Maryland to Texas and to many islands of the West Indies. Other foxtail grasses of lesser size have been introduced to America from Eurasia. They are weeds, but are plants of immense value to wild animals. Foxtail seeds held in heads high above the snow save the lives of hungry birds every winter. In the United States alone, seventy-seven different kinds of birds and mammals get a significant part of their diet from the foxtails. No other type of wild grass contributes so much.

One kind of foxtail grass has a long history of importance to mankind. It is one of five kinds of plants that the Chinese Emperor sowed each spring in a public ceremony established in 2700 B.C. This particular kind is still raised extensively as a source of grain for human use in China, Japan, Korea, and India. In Africa south of the great deserts, the plant is a weed, and its seeds are regarded as suitable only for starving people to eat. Actually the foxtail seeds are more nutritious than many more popular kinds of grain.

Over the years, cultivated foxtail grass has received many names. Foxtail millet is the commonest. Calling it a millet tells people that its seeds are edible but small (about a sixteenth of an inch long) and egg-shaped. Millet is an old

Because of a Flower

word for a small grain that can be ground up to make meal for thickening soup or porridge. In Europe, the black-seeded foxtail millet that the Chinese Emperor knew is raised as food for livestock. It is known there as Italian millet or as "black-seeded Hungarian grass." Varieties of foxtail millet with seeds of other colors bear distinctive names. Golden wonder millet, or German millet, has yellow seeds. Siberian millet, or Turkestan millet, has red or orange-colored seeds. To a wild bird or a hungry mouse, any color of millet seed is completely acceptable. In the United States and Canada, millet seeds are included in the mixture sold as "wild bird food."

Yet it is not only the seeds of the foxtail grasses that benefit animals. While its flower heads are still raised high to the breeze, birds and rabbits are making nests between the grass stems on the ground. Grasshoppers are likely to be chewing on the green leaves. Red ants may be running up and down the stems to tend the aphids they find there. These aphids gain access to rich supplies of food within the stem by piercing the plant with their slender beaks and causing the sap to flow. The grass does all the work: it makes the food, transports the nourishing solution past the tip of the aphid's beak,

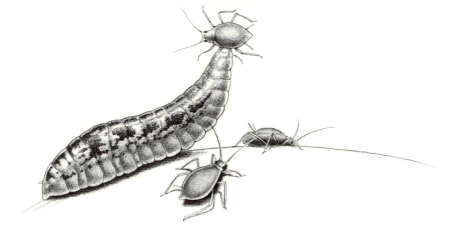

hoverfly larva, aphids

and produces enough pressure to pump the food into the insect. The aphid does not even need to suck! It gets more water and sugar than it needs. The excess comes out of the aphid through a pair of tubes and would drip to the ground if the ants were not there to lick up the sweet solution.

Unlike most animals, an aphid can reproduce without mating. During much of the summer all individuals are females. Each imbibes plant juice and grows, then gives birth to young that are tiny duplicates of herself. They crawl to the nearest vacant spot along the stem and begin getting their own sap. Quickly the aphids form a colony. Totally unarmed for defense, they are easy prey to their predators. It seems strange that the ants that come to get the sweet solution known as honeydew, fail to protect the

Because of a Flower

aphids. The ants stand aside while ladybird beetles and their voracious young attack the helpless creatures. In a few hours an entire colony of aphids may be cleared out.

The small world of the grass stem affords a living to many animals that pay no attention when a person watches through a magnifying lens. A good place to look for some action is where many aphids are taking their day-long meal of juice. Each aphid is tethered by its tubular beak to the grass stem. It cannot move easily if a predator approaches. Along comes a tiny wasp, with a body no bigger than a millet seed. The wasp is a specialist, intent on the aphids. Settling on the grass stem, the wasp runs over to the members of the colony and examines them, like a shopper at a bargain counter. The wasp, however, is not seeking the biggest aphid. A small one is better. Finding an aphid the right size, the wasp jabs the soft body with her stinger and at the same time lays an egg. The egg will hatch inside the aphid's body in a day or less, as a minute worm. It will feed on the aphid without killing it, letting the aphid grow and become bigger. Yet the aphid is doomed. The parasite is growing, too. Eventually it will bite a vital part of its host and the aphid will die. By

The Many Heads of the Foxtail Grasses

then the parasite should be ready to transform into a wasp. It escapes, becomes a wasp, and if it is a female eventually lays eggs in more aphids.

Another predator creeps among the aphids. It has a soft body, which tapers at both ends. It has no obvious head or legs, but resembles a child enclosed from the neck down in a cloth potato bag, ready to run a potato race. The creature is a maggot with a taste for aphids. The maggot approaches and taps the aphid on its back. The procedure might remind you of someone thumping a watermelon to judge its quality. If the maggot finds what it wants, it drives a pair of sharp mouth hooks into the back of the helpless aphid, lifts it aloft, and sucks out its blood. One by one in quick succession, the maggot drains its helpless victims and drops their limp bodies to the ground.

Later this maggot will transform into a graceful fly, banded in gold and black. Called a hover fly because it can stay poised in the air on quivering wings for a minute at a time, the creature shows no sign of its aggressive maggothood. It seems disinterested in grasses. It settles on flowers of other kinds and sips their nectar. Or it darts at high speed after other insects. Usually

Because of a Flower

it finds a mate. Not until a female hover fly has eggs to lay will she seek out a colony of aphids and start the cycle afresh.

So many different animals explore the grass plants in search of food for themselves or their young that a viewer can never guess which kind will turn up next. It could be a caterpillar, protectively colored to blend with the grass. Or an assassin bug, hunting for a caterpillar to pierce with a murderous beak. Or a sharp-eyed wren, seeking insects as food for young wrens in a concealed nest. The grass world is full of checks and balances. It is a whole community of green plants, of plant-eating animals and animal-eating animals, of parasites and scavengers. It fairly teems with life, most of it as inconspicuous as a grass flower.

The many heads of the foxtail grasses draw attention to plants that suit most open lands so well that they become weeds. They grow exuberantly and nourish a host of animals that otherwise might attack cultivated crops. The foxtail heads feed songbirds and give them the energy to sing. These grasses that seem useless to mankind directly keep right on flowering. They add immeasurably to the wealth of life around us.

Milkweed Flowers

> My garden is an orchestra.
> Trumpets, flutes, bright cymbals,
> flashing bows, and an audience
> of weeds.
>
> —Donald M. Murray

ALL OVER North America, schoolchildren know that the common monarch butterfly is also the milkweed butterfly. This handsome insect flies south on its black and orange wings in autumn, and north again in spring, almost like the migratory birds. Thousands of people watch for monarch butterflies that bear numbered printed paper tags. Or they raise the caterpillars on milkweed, wait until the butterflies emerge, and release the insects with tags for other people to find. This is how we know that a milkweed butterfly can travel thousands of miles; they can be found wherever milkweeds are growing.

Milkweed seeds are well equipped for traveling, too. Everyone enjoys finding a freshly split milkweed pod, with its ripe seeds exposed. One good puff in the right direction frees those seeds, each with its parachute of glistening white silky hairs. They float away on the slightest breeze.

On a dry day with a steady wind, a milkweed seed may travel a mile or more. Or it may bump into a shrub only a few feet from the pod that released it and catch there. Eventually a dash of rain wets the connection between the seed and its silken strands. Down the seed falls to the ground, perhaps at a place where it can sprout and grow.

Milkweeds can be found from the Atlantic to the Pacific, from Canada to Chile and Argentina. Some milkweeds are native to Africa south of the great deserts. All of them produce seeds with silky hairs to catch the wind. But not all milkweeds have the milky juice in their leaves, stems, roots, and flowers that gives them their name. Perhaps it would be better if we called these plants silkweeds instead of milkweeds.

Milkweed Flowers

All of the fourteen different kinds of milkweeds that monarch caterpillars eat have the milky juice. Somehow the caterpillar can bite away and swallow small pieces of the milkweed leaf without causing the leaf to bleed. Perhaps something in the saliva of the caterpillar causes the milky juice to clot and seal the wounded leaf. Even more strange is the fact that milkweed caterpillars are unharmed by the poison that most milkweeds contain. The only nourishment the caterpillars get comes from poisonous material. This seems to make them poisonous to an insect-eating bird. After tasting a monarch caterpillar or two, almost any bird will refuse to touch another caterpillar with the same appearance. As a result the caterpillars creep about unconcerned, conspicuously marked with encircling narrow bands of yellow, black, and white, and a pair of black hornlike projections at each end. Birds have no difficulty recognizing this distinctive pattern. Generally they also learn to avoid the chrysalis in which the caterpillar changes into a monarch butterfly. Even the butterfly is rarely attacked by birds. Because they can live a long time without fear of attack, they can afford to migrate from one place with milkweeds to another.

Because of a Flower

A monarch butterfly ready to lay eggs hunts for young milkweed plants. The insect recognizes the plant by scent even when it is only a few inches tall. The milkweed may be in an open field, or along a roadside, or close to the edge of a river. Or the plant may have surprised a gardener by extending first its leaves, then its stems, and finally its flowers and its seed pods from the side of a hedge.

The first sign of a milkweed plant in the spring is two pale green leaves, rising from the ground, pressed together like hands in prayer. The stout stem that supports them gets longer— 1 inch, 2 inches, 3 inches. The two leaves spread apart, each opposite the other, like twins. Between them they reveal another pair of leaves pressed together. If a mowing machine cuts off the top of the plant at this stage, it may die. The cut end bleeds profusely, dripping the same milky juice that appears from a nick in a milkweed leaf.

Allowed to grow, however, the milkweed may be 2 feet tall when summer arrives. Its flower buds appear, in clusters like tiny green grapes. The flowers in any one cluster open at almost the same time, each flower facing the sky. If you look at a single flower with a magni-

milkweed flower, pod, seeds, monarch caterpillars

fying lens, you will be looking at one of the strangest flowers in the world. But because a milkweed flower is only about a quarter of an inch across, people seldom notice how peculiar it really is.

Some milkweeds produce pale pink flowers. Other flowers are bright orange, and they open to display red parts inside. Always the flower bud resembles a small Chinese lantern, with five colorful sepals that fit together at the edges. When they spread apart, they turn downward, exposing five petals, all the same size and all spoon-shaped. The petals stand up straight, all around the flower, as if they were held in position by curving rods that come up from the center of the flower. Actually the rods are not attached to the petals, and remain after the petals fall off. Each rod supports a peculiar golden crossbar with sticky tips. The tips turn down and are concealed by the petals. These sticky tips each pick up a mass of pollen from the stamens. If you lift a crossbar out of the flower, two long lumps of golden pollen will come, too. They slide out easily from short stamens that are hidden by the petals.

As in other flowers, a bee picks up milkweed pollen by accident. The insect gets a leg caught

Milkweed Flowers

under a crossbar and pulls out a pair of pollen masses yoked together. They seem to dangle precariously on the bee's leg. Yet the strange burden usually clings to the insect and is not scraped free until the bee reaches another milkweed flower. Occasionally the system does not work. The bee gets two or three of its six legs entangled by as many crossbars, and lacks the strength to yank them loose. The insect is trapped by the flower. Unless the trapped bee gets some kind of help, it will die far from its hive. Of course, the pollen in the flower would then also go to waste.

Only a bee is likely to transfer pollen from a milkweed flower. Few other insects are attracted to these strange blossoms. Rarely does a monarch stop to seek a sip of nectar. Just occasionally some other butterfly or a fly settles to get some nourishment in this way. Many a milkweed flower, in fact, receives no pollen on its pistil. Such a flower produces no seeds, and drops off the plant. Only the few unsuccessful flowers remain.

A milkweed flower that does succeed in receiving pollen ordinarily gets a whole mass of pollen grains at once. It may produce one or two pods. The pods lengthen out as all of the

Because of a Flower

other flower parts shrivel and drop to the ground. Eventually the pod begins to swell and becomes spindle-shaped. Inside it, 150 to 200 flat seeds are growing. By the time they ripen and turn brown, the green pod that encloses them will be 3 inches long or more, and ready to split along one side. As the pod opens and lets the sun's warmth dry out the contents, the seeds lie exposed. They overlap each other like shingles on a roof and are ready for you, or the wind, to blow them to another place, where with luck they may one day sprout into new plants.

The milkweed plant is of great importance to two other kinds of insects. However, unlike the caterpillars of the monarch butterfly, these creatures bite no pieces from the leaves. Usually the leaves of a milkweed are surprisingly clean and undamaged. But on a leaf or a stem, you are likely to see a pinkish red beetle about three-quarters of an inch long. It has long black antennae and some black spots on its back. It squeaks if picked up, and may nip your fingers with its small, hard jaws. The milkweed beetle lays eggs on milkweed stems. Out of the eggs come tiny grubs that eat their way into the center of the stem. They feed there, in the soft

Milkweed Flowers

pith of stem and root, without causing the milkweed to spill any of its white juice.

Another creature, a red-and-black bug, is also often visible on a milkweed plant. It has a sucking mouth that can penetrate the plant's defenses. The milkweed bug stabs into a stem or a leaf, but not into the fine tubes that contain the milky liquid. Instead, it reaches even finer tubes through which the plant moves the sugars and other valuable products from its leaves. The bug sips directly from this rich supply. Its young act like their parents, using their shorter beaks to get food from fine veins in the leaves.

A milkweed in good health can feed a monarch caterpillar, a beetle grub or two in its pith, and a few milkweed bugs. Still the plant has nourishment to use for its own growth and for the formation of flowers and seeds. It concentrates so much goodness in its flower buds that some people collect milkweed "tops" when the buds are small, and cook them as a vegetable. Because people regard milkweeds as "just weeds," they give little thought to the fact that the topless milkweed can produce no seeds that year. Fortunately, the plant has stored nourishment in its root and survives the winter. From the root the milkweed will send up a new top with flower buds the next year.

When explorers to America first discovered milkweeds, about 275 years ago, they learned almost nothing about the way these plants contribute to the life of the fields and stream edges. They did not know that milkweed plants keep monarch butterflies—the champion migrants of the insect world—flying on their astonishing travels. Instead, the Swedish botanist who gave milkweeds their scientific name believed that the dried plants he had in his collection were native to Syria. He never realized that it was a common American weed that a Syrian was growing as a curiosity. The botanist named the plant *Asclepias syriaca*, thinking only to honor the memory of Asclepius, who is credited with being the first Greek physician. Now, scientists know better. They know, too, how many kinds of animals depend on weeds, and that the presence of the weeds makes life possible there for certain animals.

During the past century, milkweeds have been introduced in many lands where they do not grow naturally. Eventually, monarch butterflies that had lost their way arrived and found the milkweeds in these distant places. In 1845 some monarchs were caught in Hawaii, before

Milkweed Flowers

there were any milkweeds there. Monarchs reached the Marquesas Islands in the South Pacific about 1860, Australia in 1870, New Zealand in 1874, and England in 1876. Wherever the monarchs find the right kinds of milkweeds growing, they establish their kind.

Recently milkweed butterflies spread westward across the East Indies and reached Burma. No one knows whether the butterflies cross the oceans borne along on strong winds, or riding quietly aboard a ship. In many places the monarchs are called "wanderers." But their wanderings are in vain unless they find the right weeds waiting for them. Only a milkweed can feed a monarch caterpillar, or produce a milkweed flower.

Everybody's Flowers

"They are burs, I can tell you,
they'll stick where they are thrown."

—William Shakespeare (1564-1616)
Pandarus, in *Troilus and Cressida*,
Act III, Scene II.

PURPLE THISTLES, like burdocks and dandelions, are flowers of distinction. They belong to a secret community of plants that manage to accompany people almost everywhere. Their password is a special ability to thrive in bright sun, on nearly bare ground, with a minimum of water.

Originally these flowering plants came from Asia Minor. Now they flourish everywhere, beside paths and roads, in any soil that has been recently disturbed. In fields, they often grow much better than the crop plants people want.

Everybody's Flowers

They are weeds, hardy, unwanted, almost impossible to eradicate. It might be best to be content with having them, within reason, and to think of them as everybody's flowers. Most of them have some good to offer.

Already the prickly thistle is honored as the national emblem of Scotland. According to the legend, this particular weed once saved the Scots from being conquered. It was during the eleventh century A.D., after the Vikings had overrun England. A Viking soldier was creeping forward on a night attack, trying to pass the Scottish border guards. Barefoot in the darkness, he stumbled on a thistle and cried out in pain. His cry alerted the Scots, and they repelled the Vikings. Ever since, the Scots have embroidered patterns containing a thistle flower and prickly leaves on flags and clothing.

In North America, the thistle flowers offer nectar to hummingbirds, butterflies, and bumblebees. One of the most frequent visitors is the thistle butterfly, often called the painted lady. It, too, is a native of Eurasia, but now is common wherever thistles grow. It is a strong flier and migrates through the passes of the Alps at the same seasons that birds do. Thistle butterflies may have crossed the ocean to America on

painted-lady, thistles

their own wings. But more likely they concealed themselves aboard some ship and arrived without being noticed. They found thistles growing from seeds that the colonists brought as impurities in grain.

The beautiful thistle butterfly lays her eggs on thistles, or sometimes on a burdock. The caterpillars that hatch out are brownish green or gray, with narrow yellow lines lengthwise

Everybody's Flowers

and yellowish spines sticking up. As they grow larger, these caterpillars make nests for themselves. They tie together a few leaves with strands of silk and disappear from view. The caterpillar changes into a butterfly within its nest.

Ordinarily a thistle has plenty of leaves to share with a caterpillar or two. The plant goes right on growing and producing its flower buds for the year. Each bud resembles a green urn. It opens slowly to allow the purple tips of about two dozen flowers to poke out. These flowers are packed together neatly, like so many upright tubes. Partway down inside each tube is the pollen. Below the pollen is the nectar and the makings of a single seed. Until the bud opens, all of these tubular flowers are securely sealed inside. Nothing can harm them. But when the bud opens and insects are attracted to the open flowers, they are very vulnerable. Since they need pollen from another plant, however, the risk is offset by the possible gain.

Some tiny insects do climb down inside the tubular flowers and eat the pollen. Or they chew on the flower and ruin those parts that otherwise might become a seed. Or they make holes through which the plant bleeds, and then

Because of a Flower

drink up the nourishing sap. As many as half of the flowers in a thistle head may be destroyed by these attackers. But the rest have probably been pollinated by bees.

While the flowers that are left are developing their seeds, the stiff green parts that concealed the flowers in the bud close again partway. All that is exposed at the tip is white fluff made of fine hairlike projections from the top of each ripening seed. These projections can spread apart later and form a sort of parachute. The wind can catch them and pull the seed out of the head, then carry it away.

The appearance of those hairlike projections from a thistle head is an event for which the goldfinches have been waiting. These agile little birds, smaller than a sparrow, are the last each year to start building a nest and raising a family. Not until the goldfinches can find thistledown to use as a soft lining for the nest will the male and the female get to work. Soon the two make repeated trips to thistle plants. The male is particularly easy to see because of his butter-yellow feathers, his black cap, his black wings with white bars. His mate wears inconspicuous plumage, mostly different shades of greenish yellow. Both partners fly at high speed on an undulating course, as though riding a roller coaster. Their excited calls sound like *potato-chip* or just *whee-ee-ee!*

Sometimes a goldfinch carries so much thistledown on a trip from the plant to its nest that it can scarcely see where it is flying. But the bird still goes, at almost 20 miles an hour. Often some of the thistledown has a seed or two attached. If the seeds break off during the flight, they fall and have a chance to sprout and produce new thistles. If, however, the seeds are taken into the nest, the goldfinch is likely to eat them while spreading out the thistledown. Goldfinches eat small seeds of many kinds, and later choose very soft ones to carry to their nestlings.

In late summer, the young goldfinches begin following their parents, learning to find seeds for themselves. By then the thistle seeds have all been eaten or scattered. Yet other seeds are plentiful. Goldenrod and asters provide countless millions of them. The days are getting shorter, the nights longer. This change influences the dandelions. All through the long summer days they have produced almost no flowers or seeds. Now they start to blossom again and add to the abundance that greets the gold-

Because of a Flower

finches. One kind of seed these birds rarely seek out, however, is the seed of the burdock plant. Although the flower heads of a burdock resemble in miniature those of a thistle, their edible seeds are well protected. Around them is a wall of dry, sharp hooks.

Even the burdock flowers, while they are open, are surrounded by hooks, stiff and green. The hooks form a cup from which the tips of the flowers in the head extend. Each flower is tubular, with five narrow petals joined together. From the tube, five tiny stamens extend to release white pollen. Small bees come to gather the nectar and pick up the pollen, just as bigger bees visit the thistle flower head. But a burdock produces no thistledown. It gets its small hard seeds distributed in a different way.

Each flower head of a burdock breaks off easily from the plant. When the seeds are ripe, the hooks of the flower head catch on clothing or on the fur of any passing animal. Off comes the flower head, to become the burr of the burdock. It clings to whatever it has become attached to until it is scraped off somewhere else. Snow or rain will later wet the burr and make the flower head fall apart. Even if a bird or a mouse finds the seeds that spill out, and eats

burdock bur

most of them, one or two may remain. They sprout and produce new burdock plants.

In its first year, a burdock consists only of a few coarse leaves and a deep root. The next year the burdock will use the food that it stored in its deep taproot to grow tall. It will send up a branching stem that may reach 10 feet. Each branch will offer a cluster of flower heads to attract the attention of flying insects.

Some people watch for burdock plants that are beginning to grow upward in their second year. Carefully these people dig out the thick root, which resembles a cream-colored carrot. It can be cooked and eaten. So can the young plant if it is allowed to grow a foot tall. Not until later will it become tough and fibrous. And if coffee is not available, a substitute can be made by grinding burdock seeds. A burdock

Because of a Flower

is a very useful weed for anyone who has more time than money.

A dandelion is useful, too, and not just as food for a pet rabbit. The taproot of a dandelion can be dug, dried, roasted, ground, and used as a substitute for coffee. In spring the young leaves of the plant can serve as salad greens, or be cooked as a vegetable at least as flavorful as spinach. Later the leaves become too tough and bitter.

Dandelions waste no energy in producing stems. Rather, each plant extends a circle of leaves to catch the sunlight, and sends up hollow stalks tipped by green buds. The bud opens to reveal a head of golden yellow flowers—a whole bouquet at once. Often the dandelion flowers are among the first to announce the arrival of spring.

A young dandelion, with only a few small leaves, may produce only a flower head or two. An older plant, which already possesses a dense rosette of larger leaves, is likely to open several flower heads each day for a week or two. The flower heads on all dandelions, young or old, are about an inch or so in diameter. Just big enough to attract honeybees and other insects. Early in the season, the dandelion flowers may be almost the only ones a bee can find as a source of nectar and pollen. The bee fairly wallows among the flowers in each dandelion head. Later the insect combs the pollen from the hairs on its body, and uses it to make "bee bread" for immature bees.

Scientists have discovered that dandelion pollen is sterile. The plant gains nothing from having insects visit its flowers, for it produces seed anyway. Yet the plant follows an inherited routine. It opens each flower head soon after the sun rises, on several days in succession. It closes the flower head in midafternoon, or earlier if clouds come over. Generally the yellow petals are more orange and slightly tattered on the last day the head will open. These heads are ideal for making yellow dye with which to color eggs for holidays. The recipe calls for one and one-half cups of flower heads. Pour over them a cup of boiling water and let them steep for several minutes. Strain out the flowers and add a teaspoonful of vinegar. Then dye the eggs immediately by dipping them in the hot liquid until they are the right color.

After that final day, the flower head of a dandelion closes and stays closed. Now the plant fills the seed each flower is making with

Because of a Flower

sugar, and transforms the sugar into starch within the seed itself. People often collect recently closed flower heads by the thousand, and use them as a source of sugar for making dandelion wine.

If nothing harms the flower head, its green covering eventually falls away. The seeds made by each flower are revealed and a little tuft of silken hairs spreads out at the pointed tip of each ripe seed. Together these hairs form a delicate "blowball" as much as 2 inches in diameter. They are ready to catch the wind and fly off to make more dandelions. But instead, they may attract goldfinches and other small birds that peck through the hairs and seize the seeds as food. More often a breeze picks up the hair tufts like parachutes and wafts the seeds away. Or a child provides the wind. With a huff and a puff, the child blows most of the seeds away. Those that remain are counted. Sometimes the number of them corresponds exactly to the hour of day. Could it be that ten or eleven of them are normally still firmly attached in the late morning, and all but two or three are ready to go by early afternoon?

Dandelions, burdocks, and thistles are just some of the weeds that everyone recognizes

Everybody's Flowers

when they are in flower. Nobody objects to seeing them picked, for plenty more are always left. They are everybody's flowers.

Flowers Everywhere

> After battle, flowers.
> And in the crack
> of city sidewalk,
> country bloom.
>
> —Donald M. Murray

EVERYWHERE that flowering plants grow, they brighten the world and make it a more lively place. And everywhere the flowers attract animals or put the wind to work. The plant stays rooted in the soil while its pollen grains go traveling.

Each kind of flowering plant has its own inherited way to form flowers and expose them. It comes into bloom at a definite season. It offers nectar and pollen only at certain times of the day. This inherited program is successful only where it matches the customary climate

Flowers Everywhere

and weather and soil of the area where the plant is growing. This is why each part of the world has its distinctive flowering plants.

The whole world has so many thousand different kinds of flowers that no one can ever meet them all. Yet, with a little practice and experience, anyone can learn to recognize a great many different families of flowering plants wherever they grow. Color is less important than the shape of the flower parts and the way they spread apart to give access to the pollen. We recognize a daisy, whether it is a white marguerite in New England or a bright magenta in South Africa.

The local animals that visit flowers notice color as well as shape. They conserve their energy by going from one blossom to another of the same kind. They are more likely to find a reward for each visit by working similar flowers. Both the kind of daisy and the kinds of insect visitors will be different in New England from South Africa. But the way the flower attracts the local insects and the way they respond is the same—because it is a daisy.

Each flower forms a center in the community of nature where it grows. Small animals, such as insects, come from far away because they

Because of a Flower

can see the flower or smell it. Their presence attracts the larger birds and beasts of prey. While the larger animals wait for a victim on which to pounce, they contribute wastes that nourish the roots of the plant.

The flowers fade, but fruits and seeds ripen. These appeal to animals of quite different kinds —the fruit-eaters and the seed-eaters. These animals travel to the plant to get what it offers. The plant again becomes a center of attraction. And in turn, it benefits from its visitors, for they transport its seeds and fertilize its roots.

Every flowering plant offers something that benefits other kinds of life. The blossom may be barely as big as a pinhead, like those of the water-meal—a minute plant that floats on the surface of quiet streams and ponds. Or the blossom may be 3 feet across, like those of the *Rafflesia* plant that grows as a parasite on vine roots in the rain forests of Malaya. Whatever its size or wherever it lives, it is never really alone. It attracts many other creatures that live near it and come close.

According to what the flowering plant is and where it grows, it appeals to a particular set of animals. They may be denizens of a river or a shallow pond. They may live in a marsh or

Flowers Everywhere

swamp, a forest or grassland, a desert or on a mountain slope. Every part of the world (except the oceans, the deep waters, and the great glaciers) has its flowering plants and attendant animals.

Everywhere, people and many wild creatures enjoy flowers and the fruits from flowers. And everywhere, everyone can enjoy exploring the small worlds around these plants that exist *Because of a Flower*.

For Further Reading

Grant, Karen A., and Grant, Verne. *Hummingbirds and Their Flowers*. New York and London: Columbia University Press, 1968.

Grant, Verne. "The Fertilization of Flowers." *Scientific American*, June 1951.

Heinrich, Bernd. "The Energetics of the Bumblebee." *Scientific American*, April 1973.

Martin, Alexander C., Zim, Herbert S., and Nelson, Arnold L. *American Wildlife and Plants*. New York, London and Toronto: McGraw-Hill Book Co., 1951.

Milne, Lorus J., and Milne, Margery. *Living Plants of the World*. New York: Random House, 1967.

Pijl, L. van der, and Dodson, C. H. *Orchid Flowers: Their Pollination and Evolution*. Coral Gables, Florida: University of Miami Press, 1967.

Flowers in the Text

apple, 21
artichoke, Jerusalem, 67–68
aster, 139

blackberry, 11, 23–34
burdock, 140–42, 144
buttercup, 6

cacao, 58–59
cactus, 21, 97–110
calla lily, 16–17
cattelya orchid, 60–61
cereus, night-blooming,
   13–14
cholla, 102–4
Christmas cactus, 98–99
clover, 21
columbine, 20
cow lily, 44–46

daisy, 16, 70–71, 147
dandelion, 13, 16, 139,
   142–45
dicots, 17–18
dove flower, 59–60

four-o'clock, 13
foxtail grass, 116–22

goldenrod, 21, 139
grass, 111–22

lady's-slipper, 49, 52–53
larkspur, 20
lily, 16–17
lotus, American, 47–48
   sacred, 46–47

magnolia, 8–9, 16

milkweed, 123–33
millet, 117–18
monocots, 17–18
morning glory, 13, 17

oak, 21, 84–96
orchid, 17, 49–61

peach, 10
poinsettia, 16–17
prickly pear, 99–104

Rafflesia, 148

saguaro, 106–7
skunk cabbage, 14

snapdragon, 17
squash, 17
strawberry, 11–12
sunflower, 62–71

thistle, 16, 134–39, 144
tulip, 6, 17
tuliptree, 16

vanilla, 56–59

water lily, 13, 21, 35–48
water lotus, 46–48
water meal, 148

yucca, 72–83